MANDALA FUN
Adult Coloring Book
Volume 1

By Cheryl Colors
#cherylcolors
www.facebook.com/cherylcolors

www.adultcoloringworldwide.com
https://globaldoodlegems.wordpress.com/

Copyright © 2016 Cheryl Colors
All rights reserved.
Published by Global Doodle Gems and Adult Coloring Worldwide
ISBN-13: 978-8793449084 / ISBN-10: 8793449089

Cover page, editing and formatting by #anniecolors

··· DEDICATION ···

This book is dedicated to all the wonderful artists of Adult Coloring Worldwide
who gave inspiration to colorists around the globe,
and to all the administrators who have stuck by to continually share
and inspire those who love to color.

Thank You: Angela, Jolene, Missy, Kristin, Brandy, Tracy, and Annie
www.facebook.com/angelacolorz
www.facebook.com/Joleneforartfulcoloring
www.facebook.com/MissyColorsWW
www.facebook.com/anniecolorsworldwide

LET'S GET COLORING!!

• USE THIS PAGE TO TEST YOUR COLORS •

Tip: Extra blank sheets located at the back of this book can be torn out and placed underneath your coloring pages can help to prevent bleed-through when coloring.

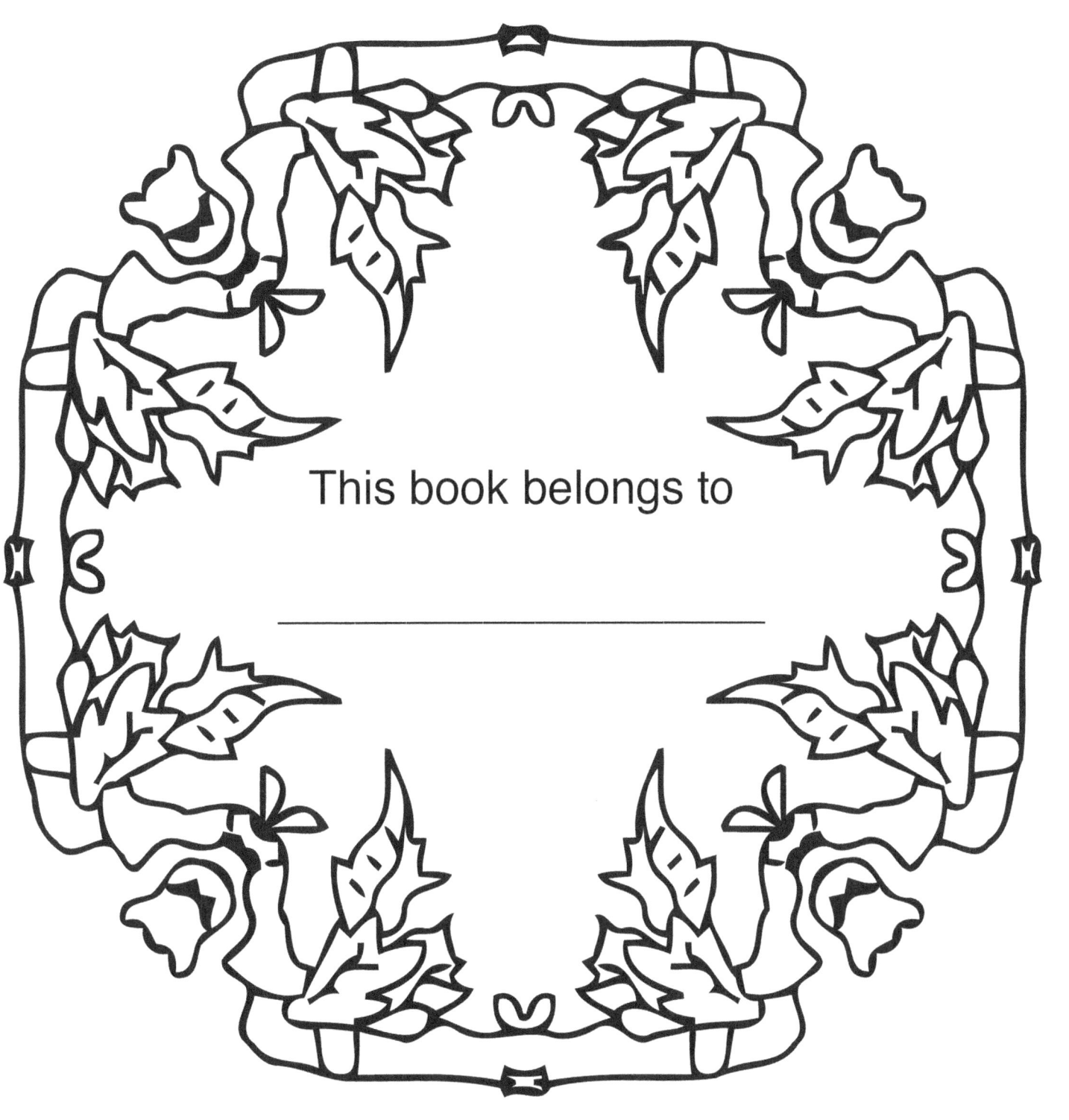

MANDALA FUN
Adult Coloring Book Volume 1

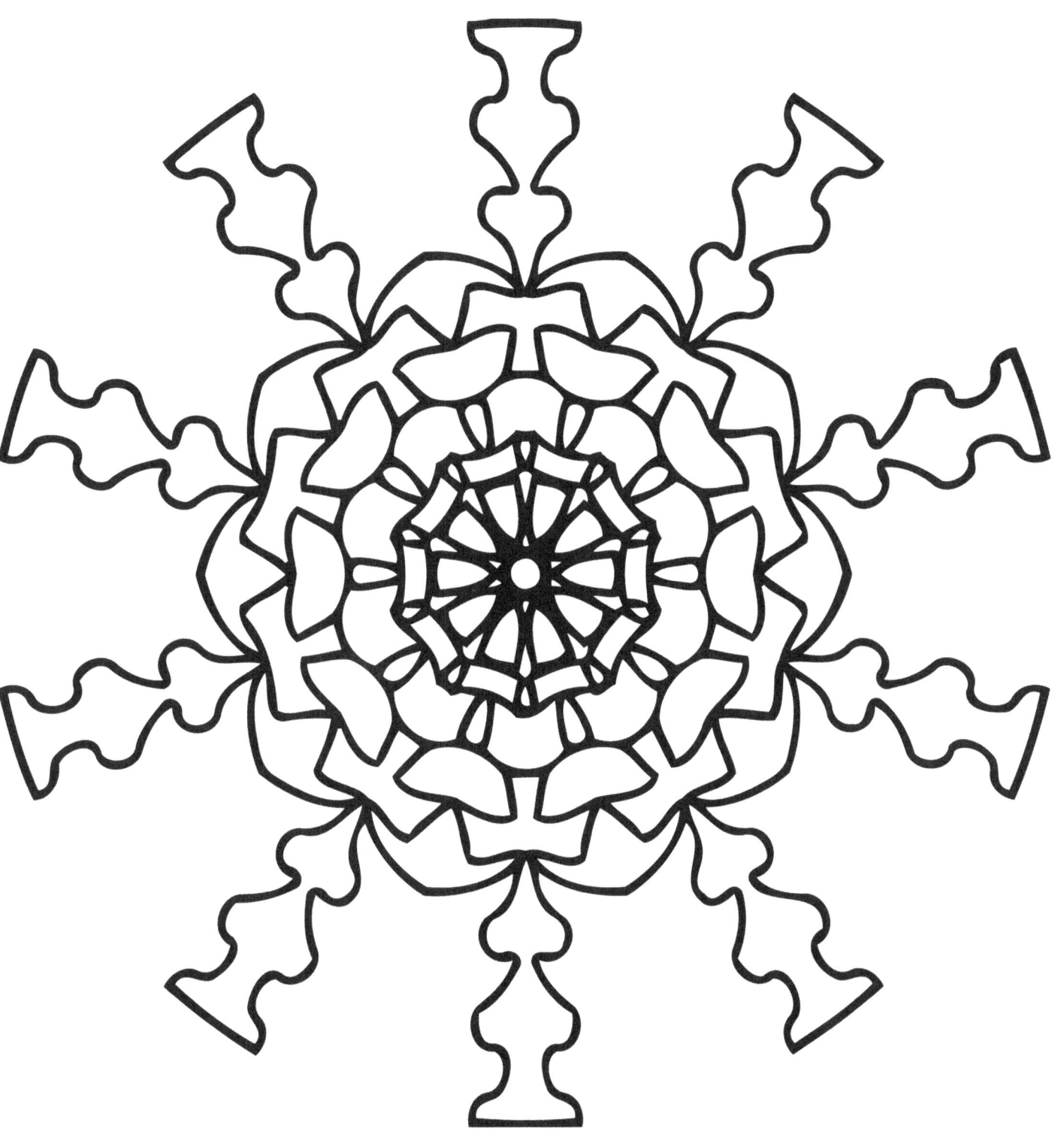

Illustrated by #cherylcolors
www.facebook.com/cherylcolors

Colored by: _____

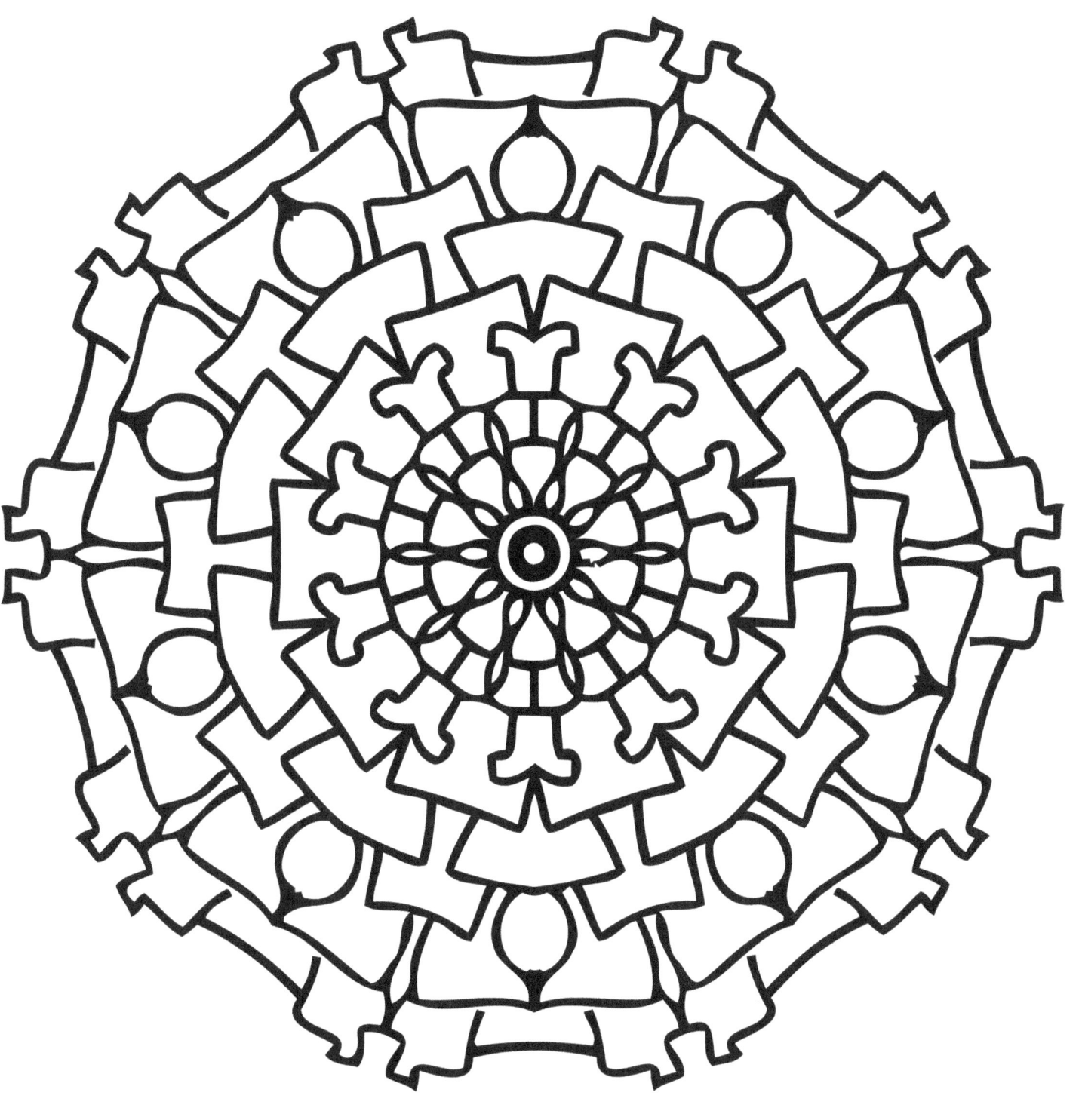

Illustrated by #cherylcolors
www.facebook.com/cherylcolors

Colored by: _____

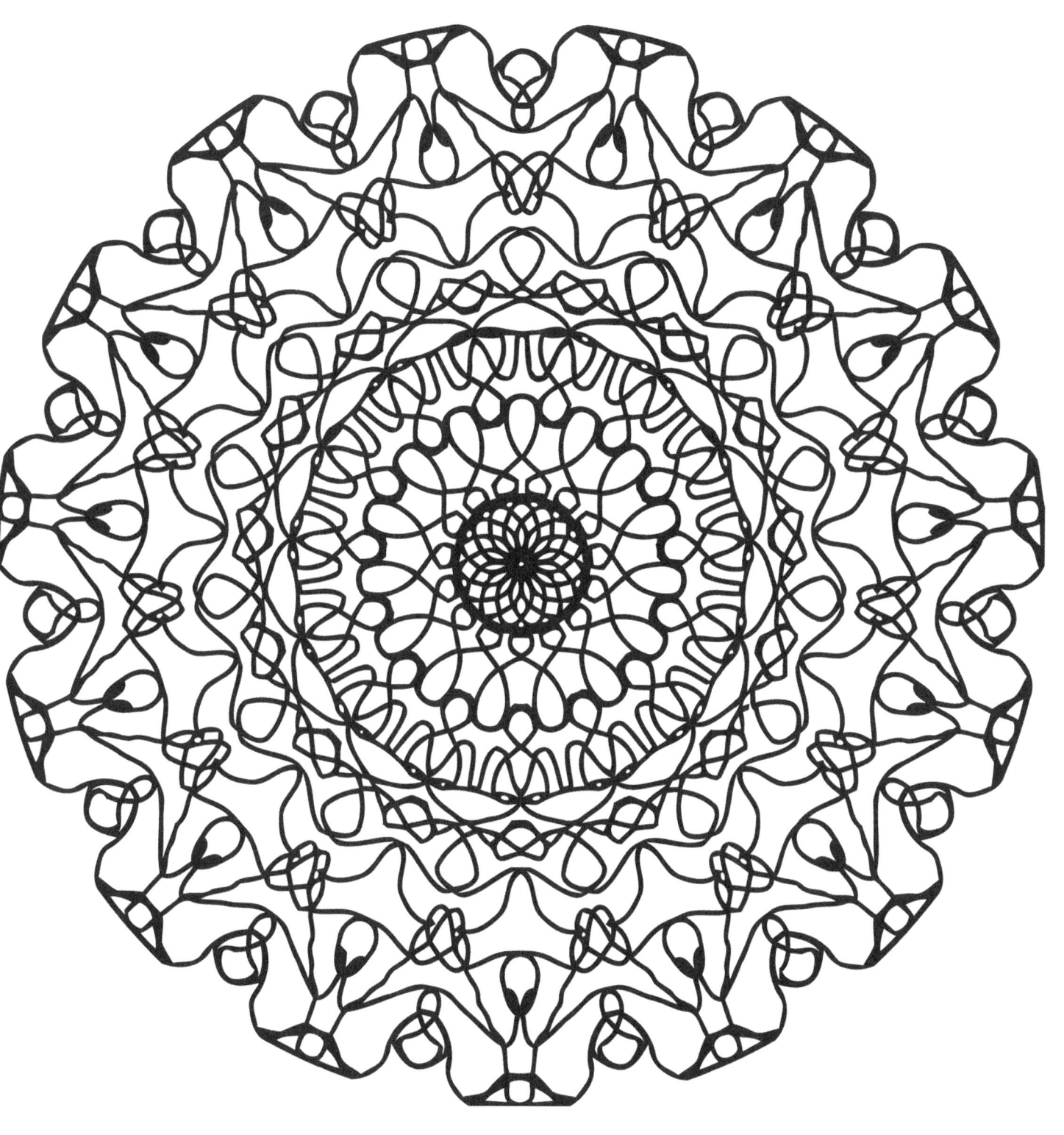

Illustrated by #cherylcolors
www.facebook.com/cherylcolors

Colored by: _____

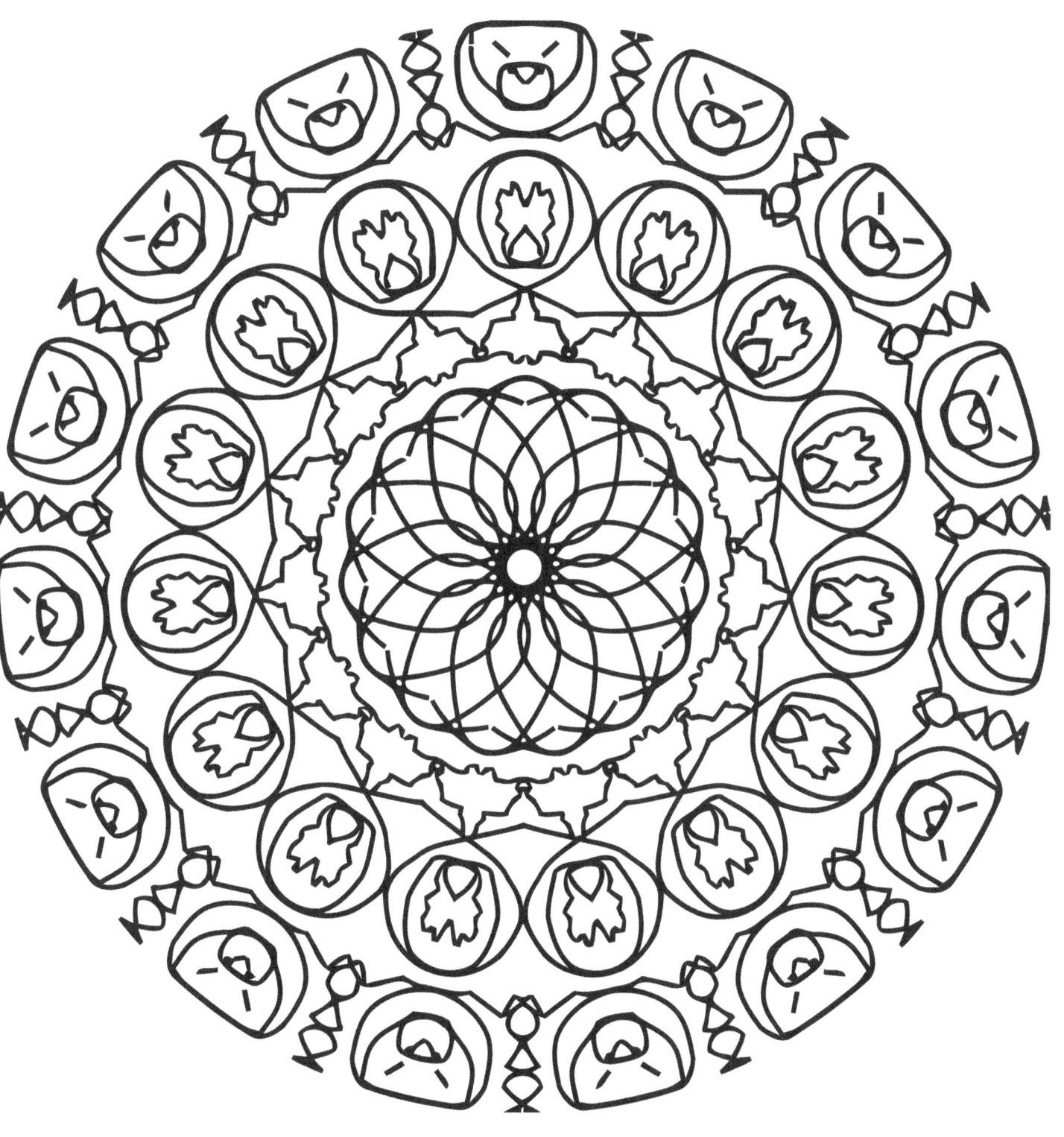

Illustrated by #cherylcolors
www.facebook.com/cherylcolors

Colored by: _____

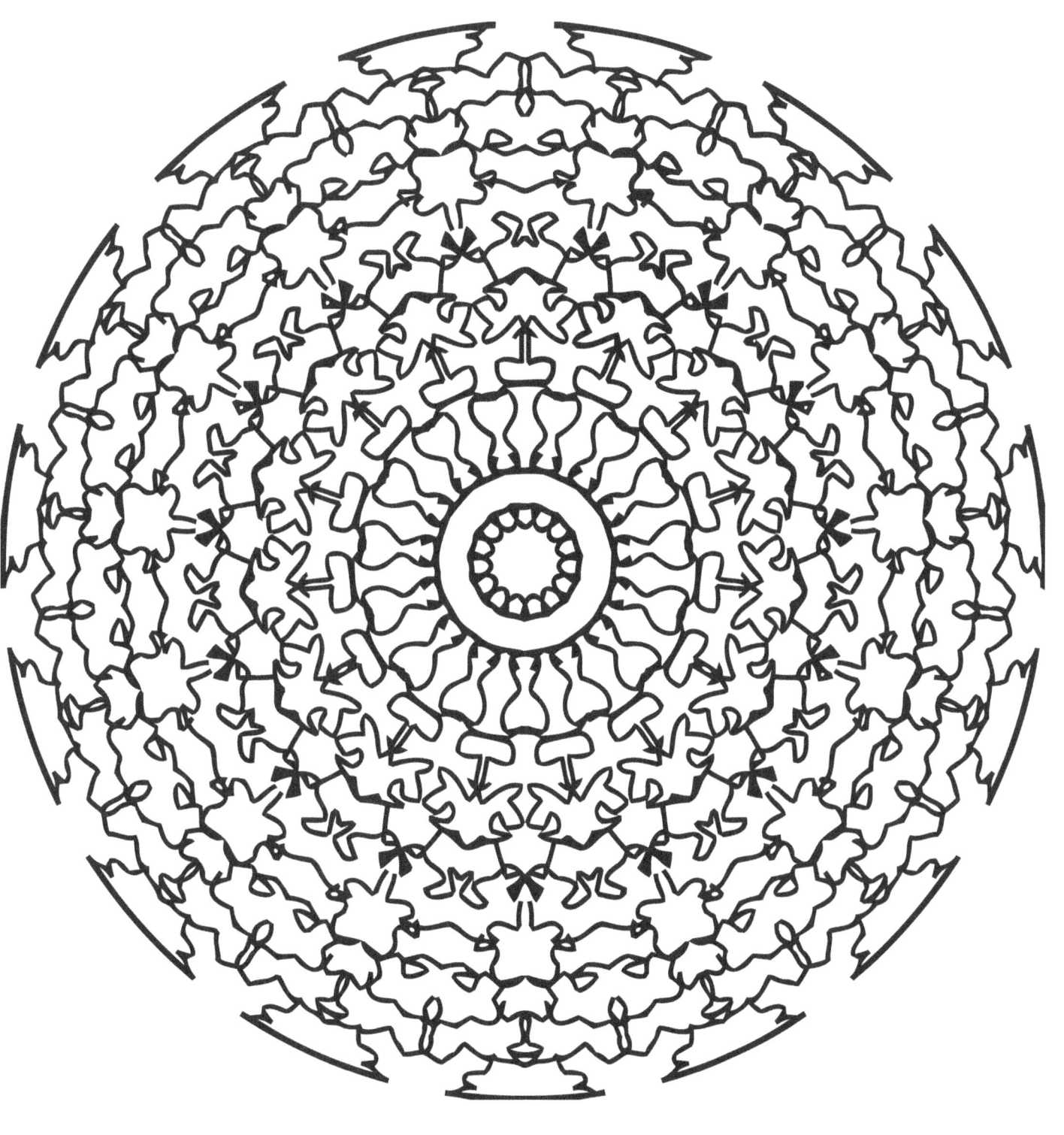

Illustrated by #cherylcolors
www.facebook.com/cherylcolors

Colored by: _____

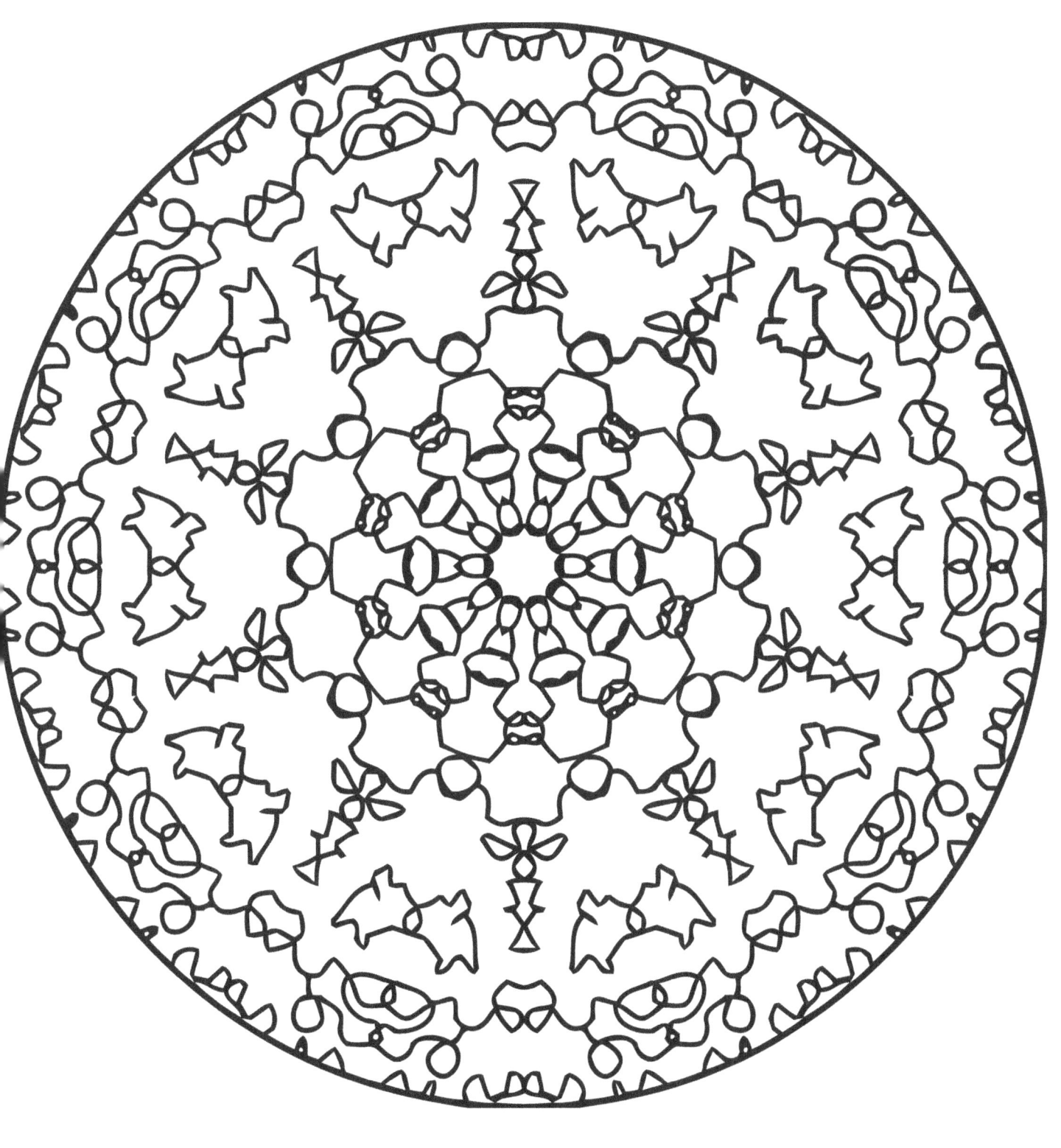

Illustrated by #cherylcolors
www.facebook.com/cherylcolors

Colored by: _____

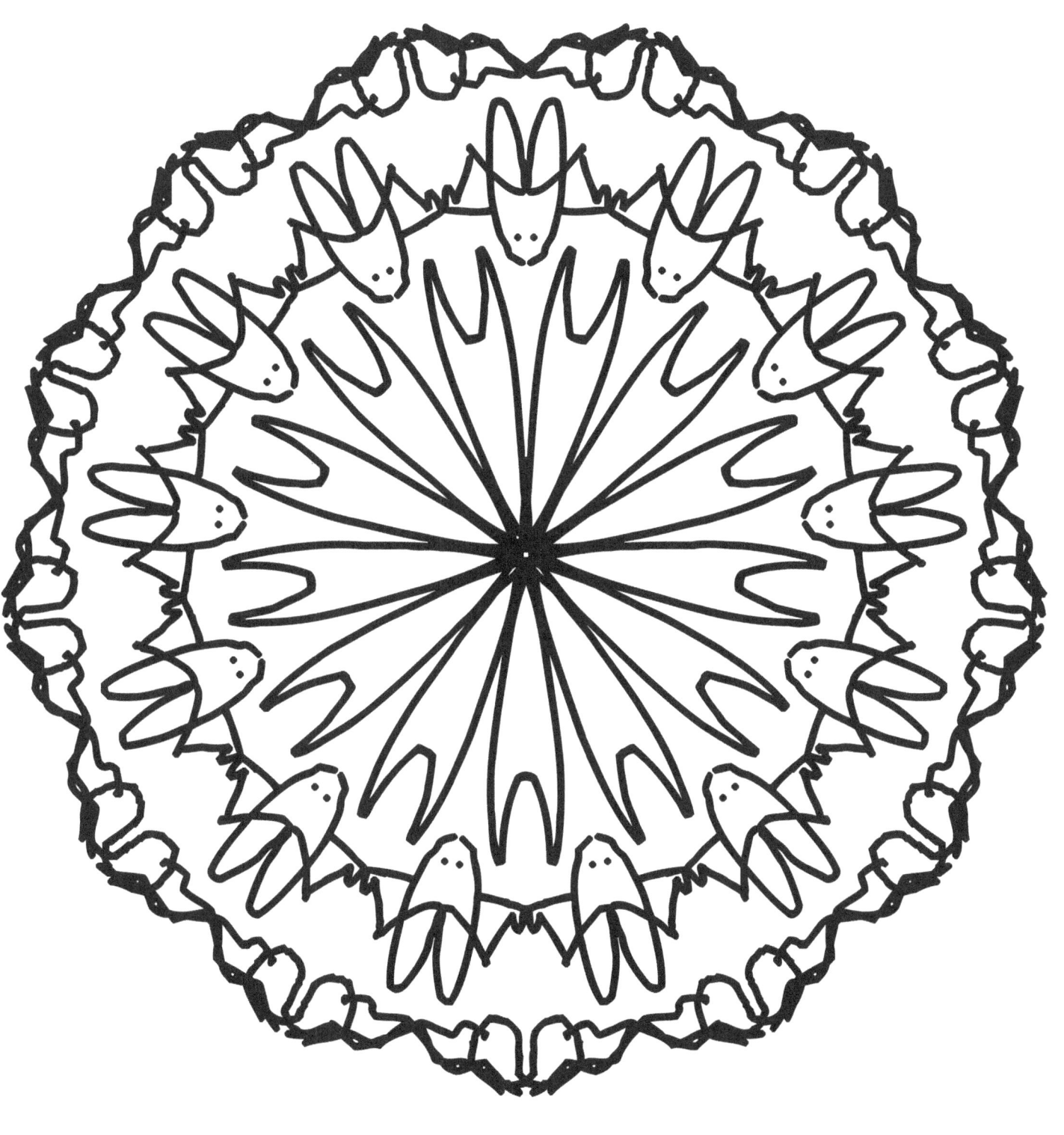

Illustrated by #cherylcolors
www.facebook.com/cherylcolors

Colored by: _____

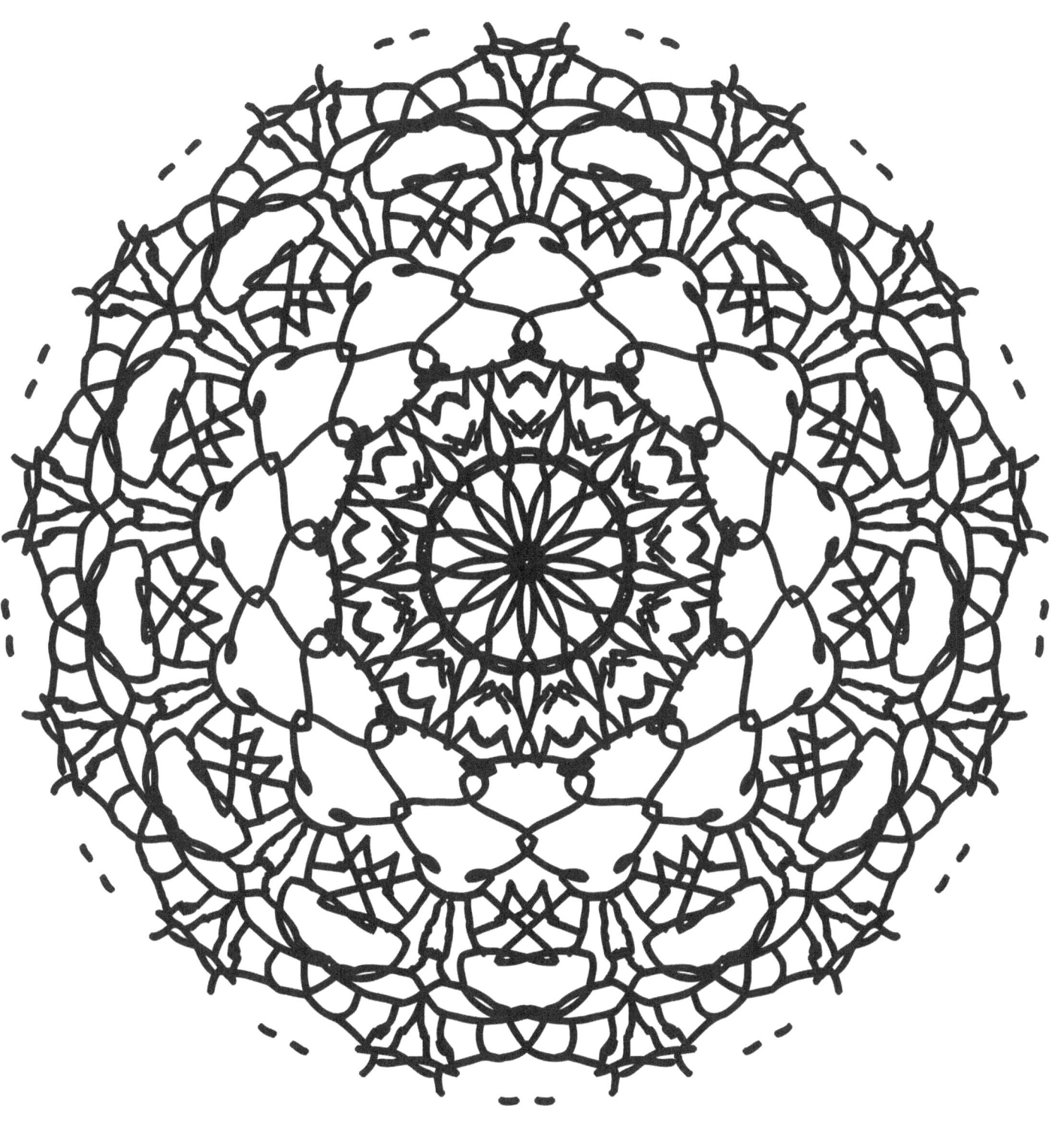

Illustrated by #cherylcolors
www.facebook.com/cherylcolors

Colored by: _____

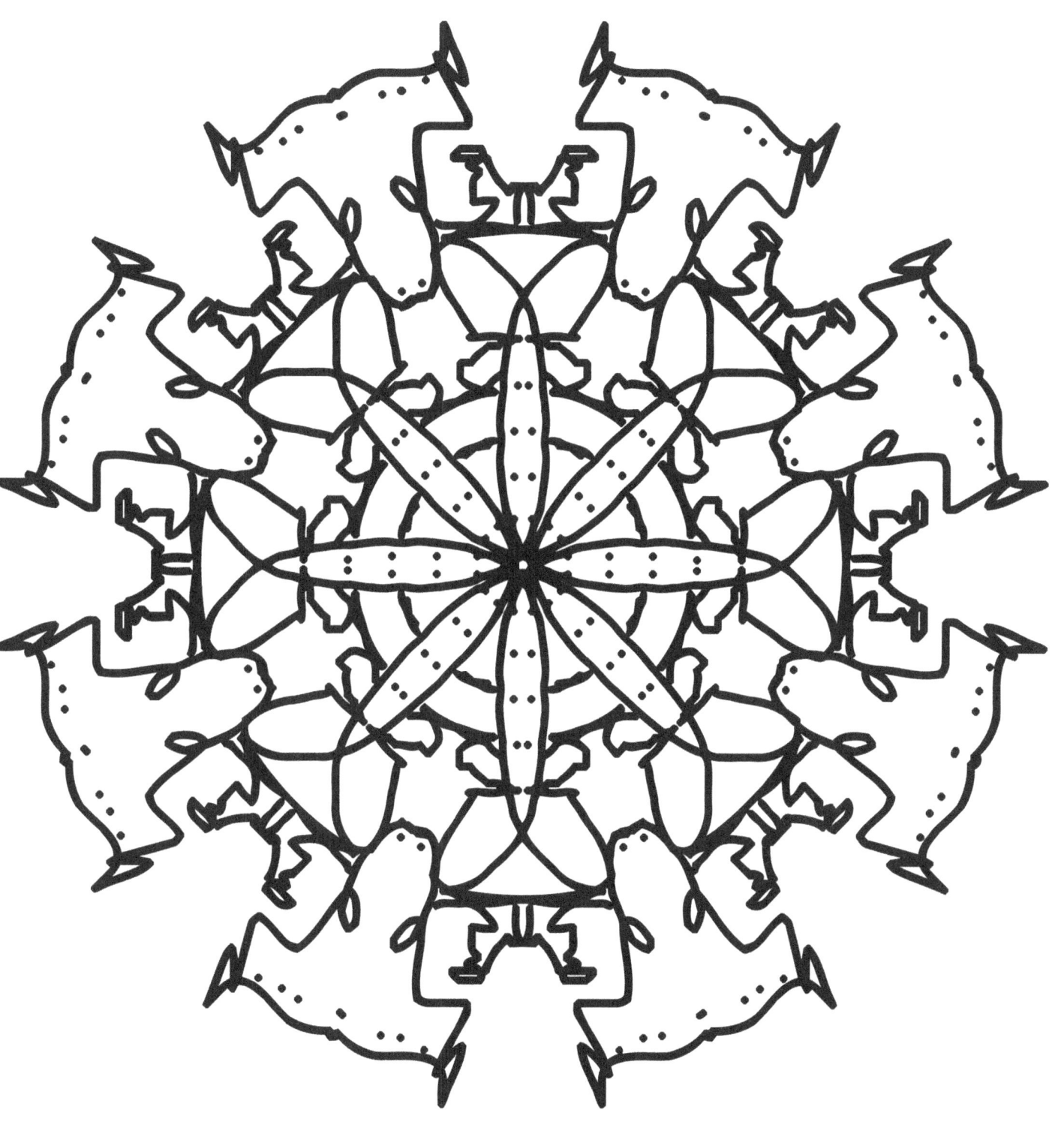

Illustrated by #cherylcolors
www.facebook.com/cherylcolors

Colored by: _____

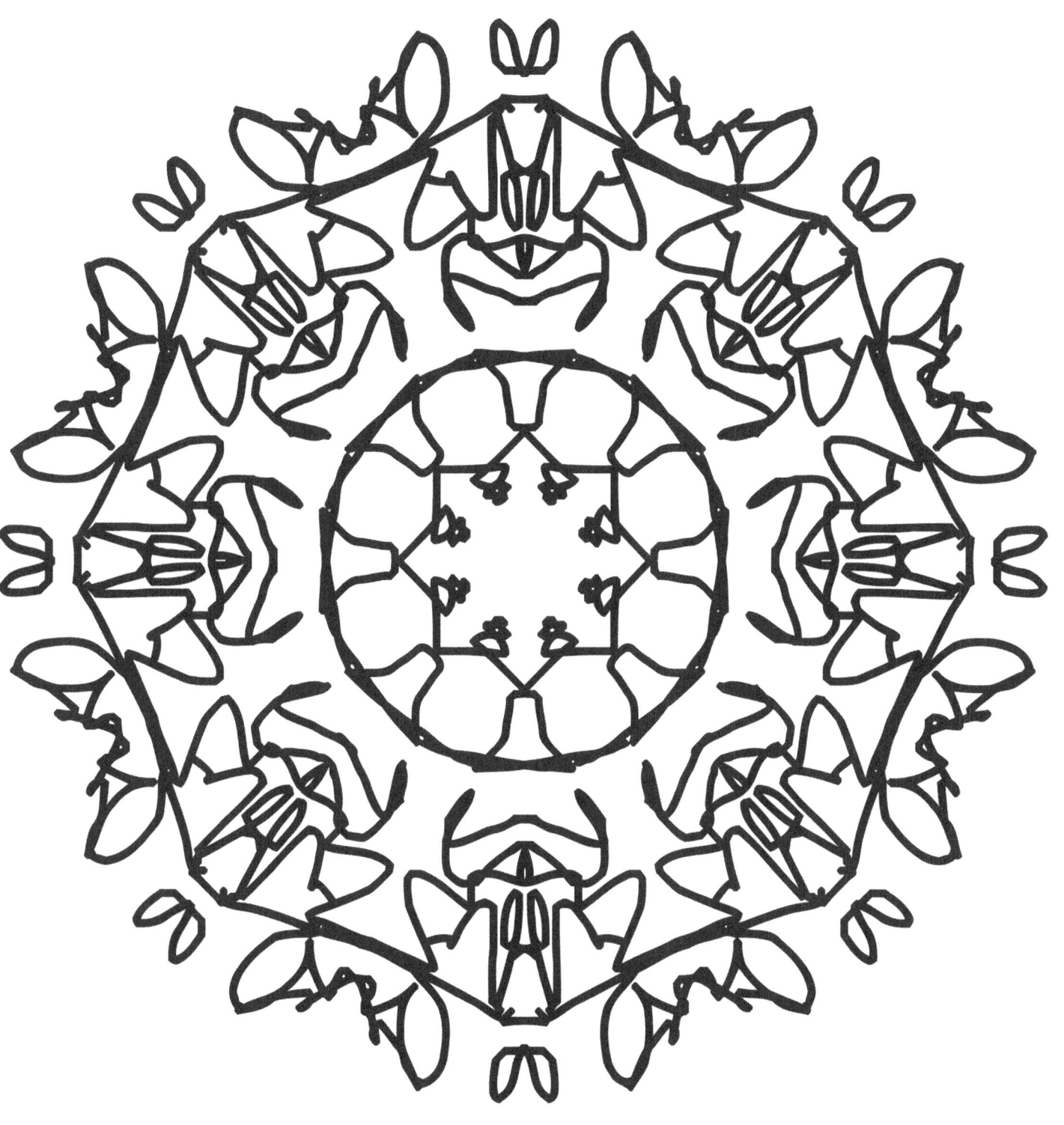

Illustrated by #cherylcolors
www.facebook.com/cherylcolors

Colored by: _____

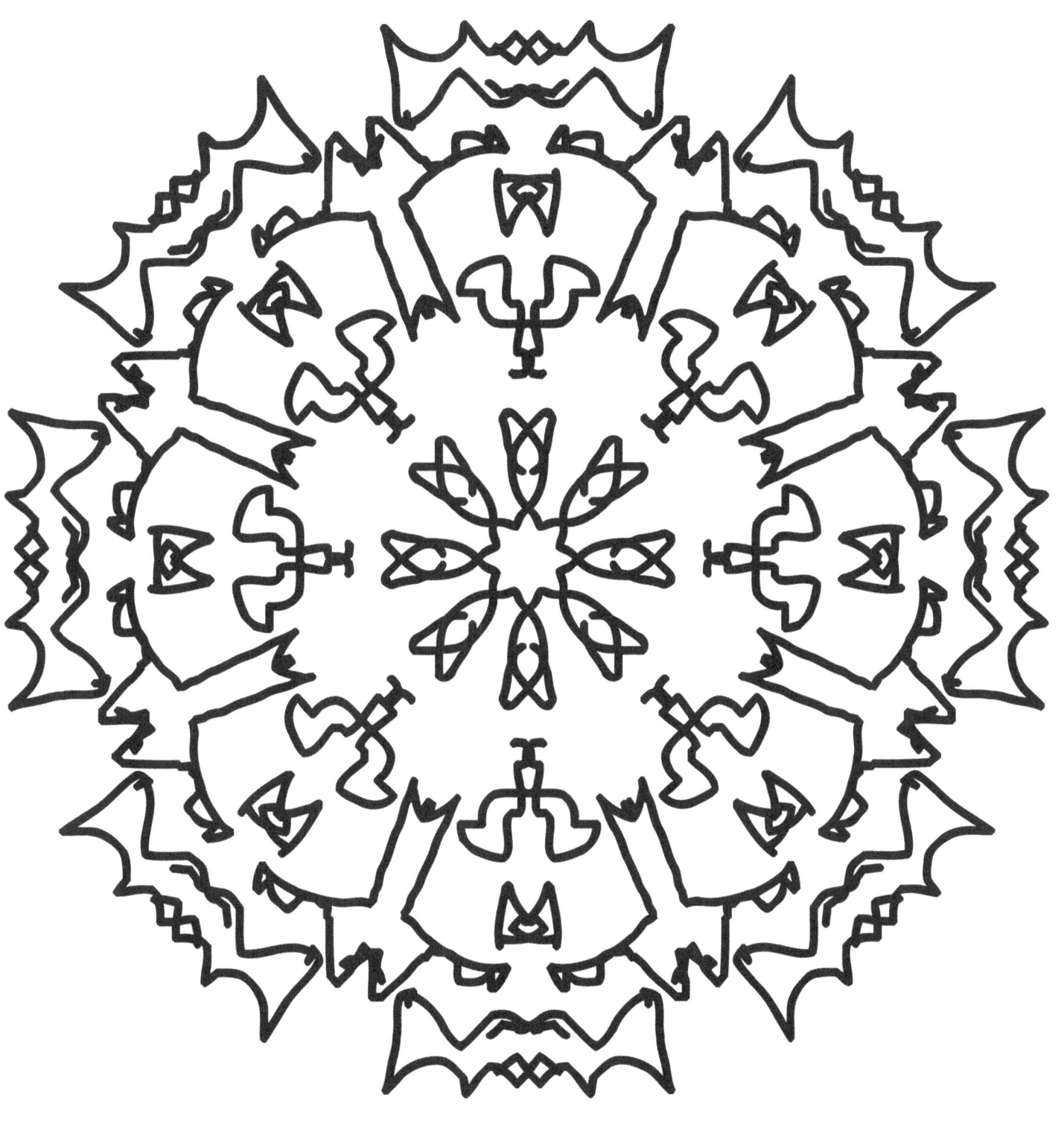

Illustrated by #cherylcolors
www.facebook.com/cherylcolors

Colored by: _____

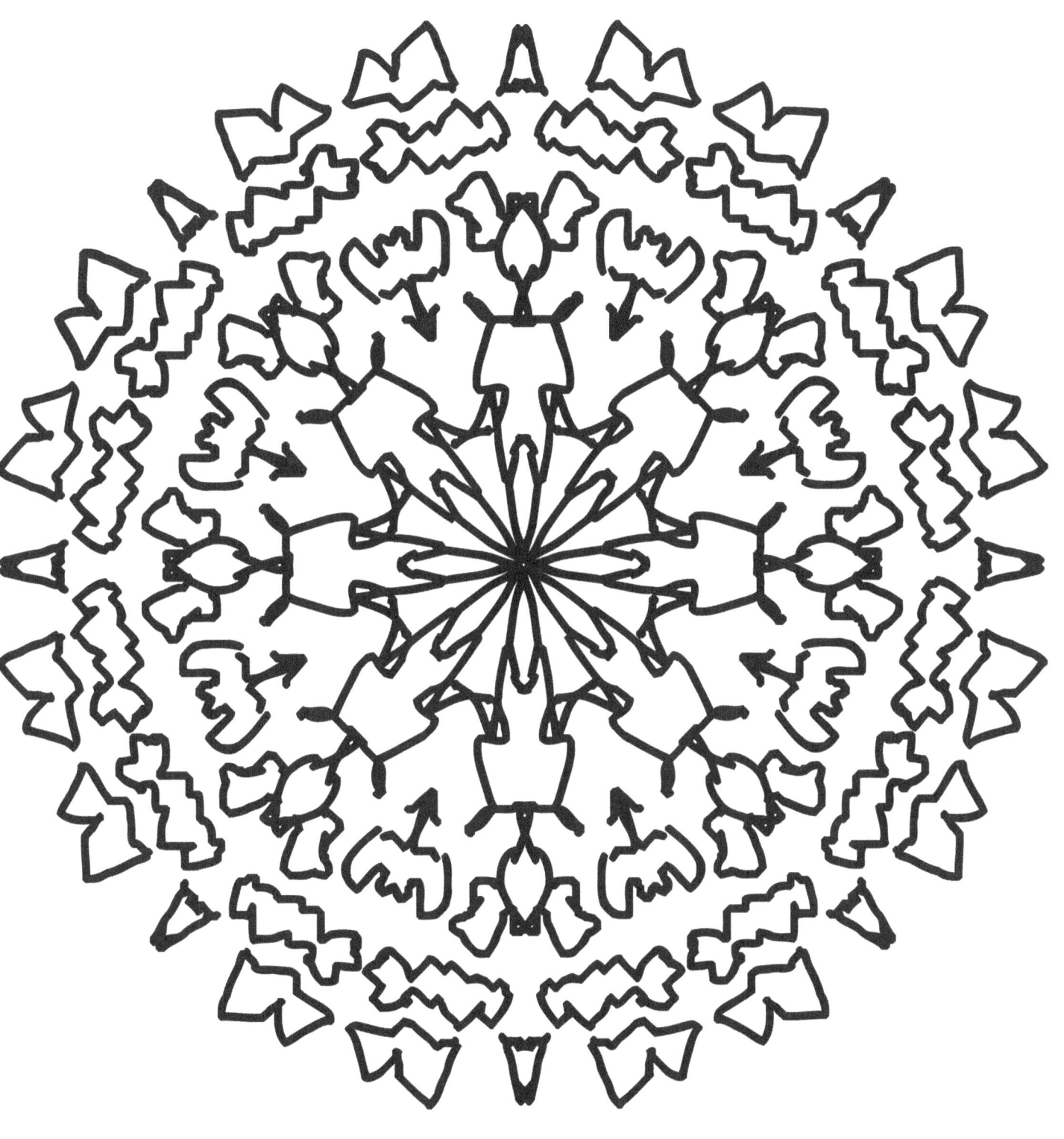

Illustrated by #cherylcolors
www.facebook.com/cherylcolors

Colored by: _____

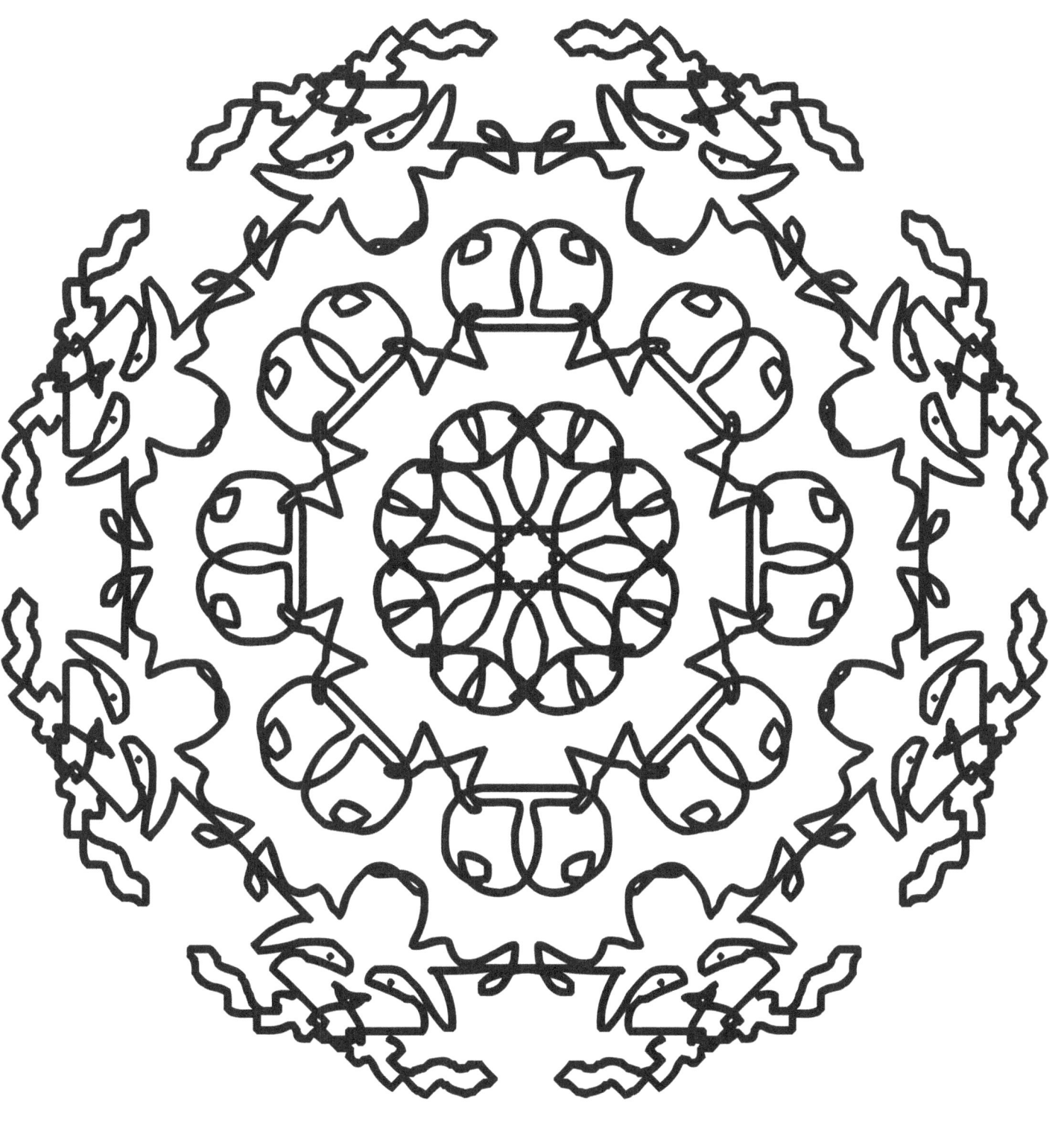

Illustrated by #cherylcolors
www.facebook.com/cherylcolors

Colored by: _____

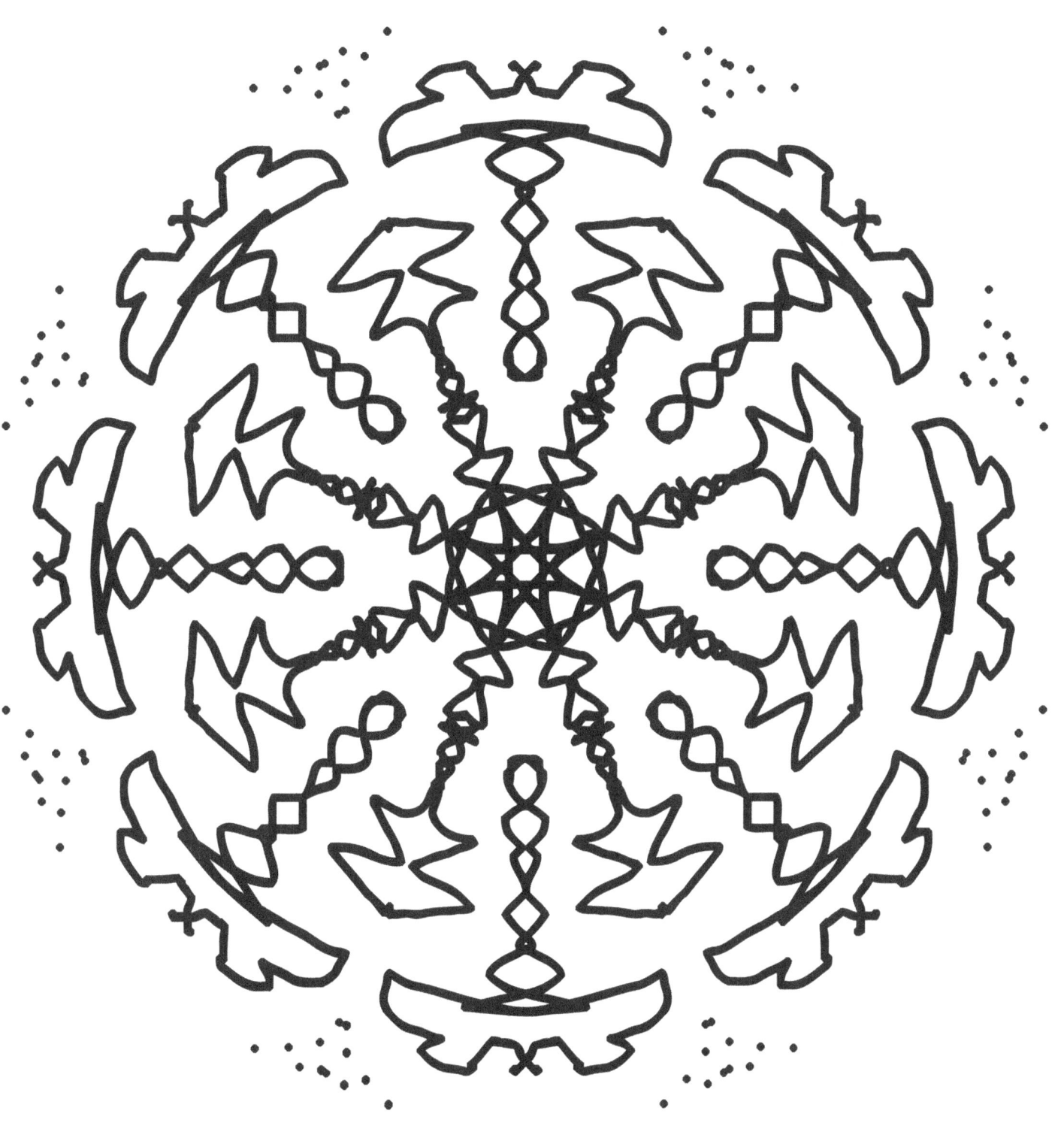

Illustrated by #cherylcolors
www.facebook.com/cherylcolors

Colored by: _____

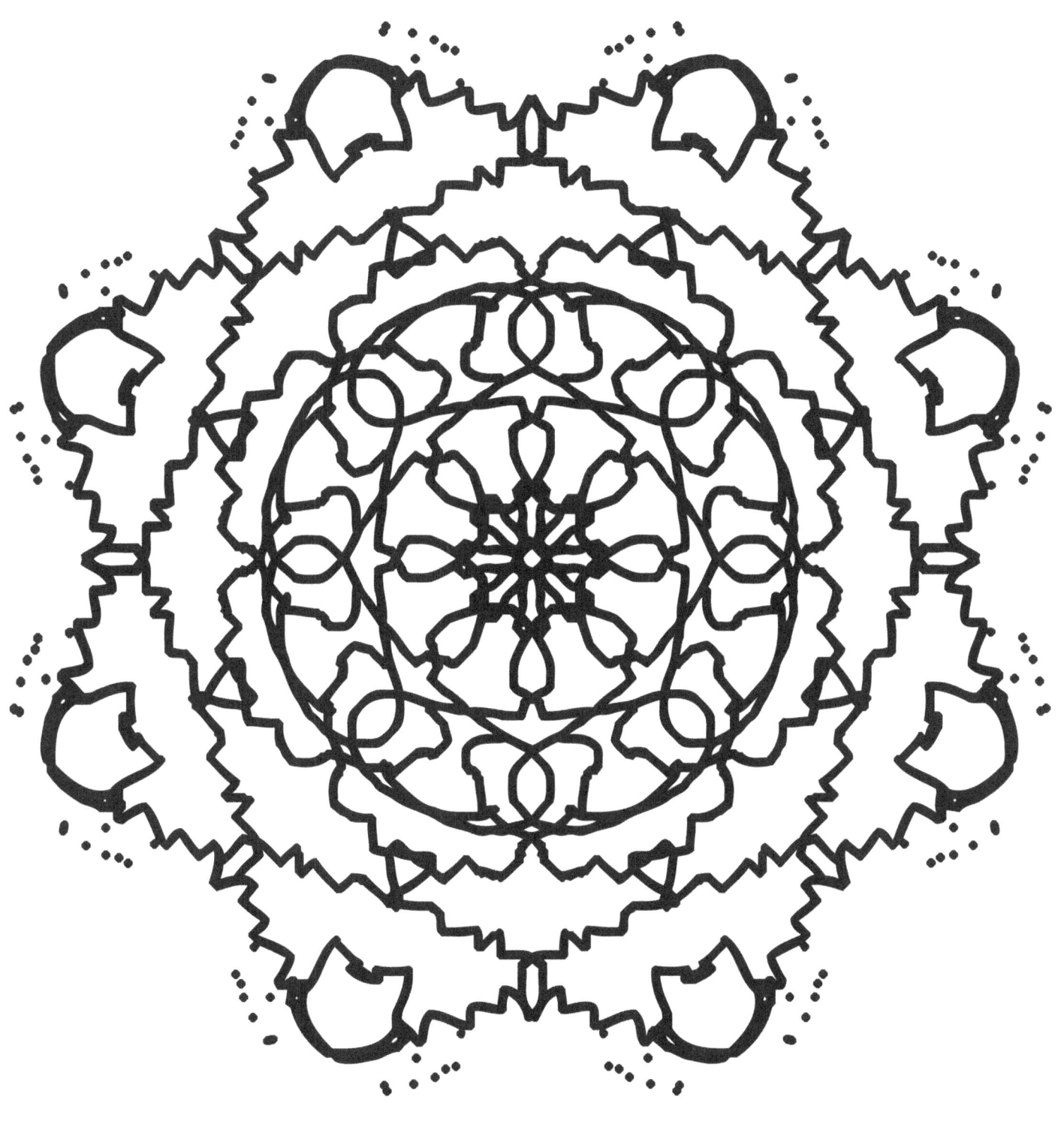

Illustrated by #cherylcolors
www.facebook.com/cherylcolors

Colored by: _____

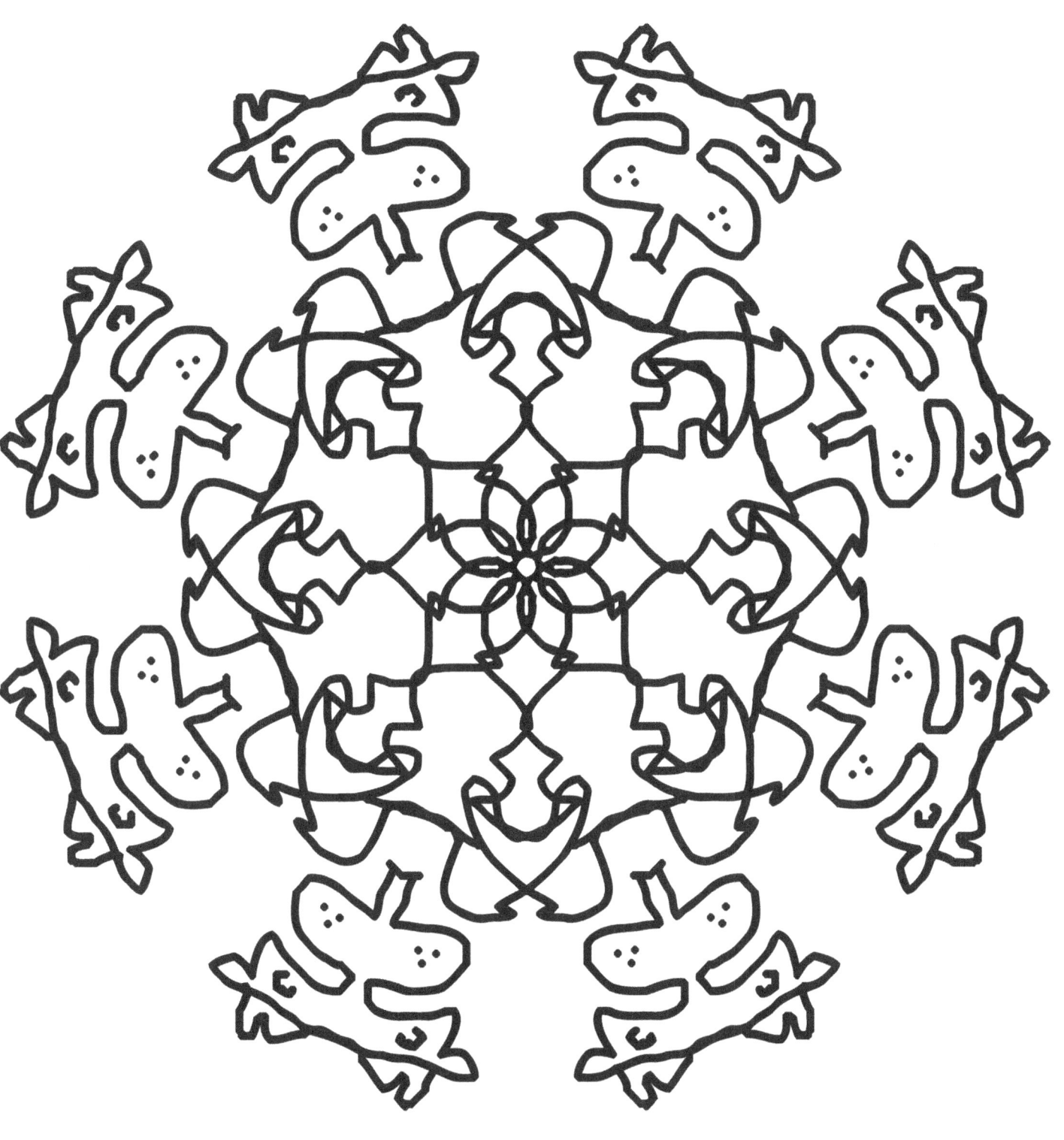

Illustrated by #cherylcolors
www.facebook.com/cherylcolors

Colored by: _____

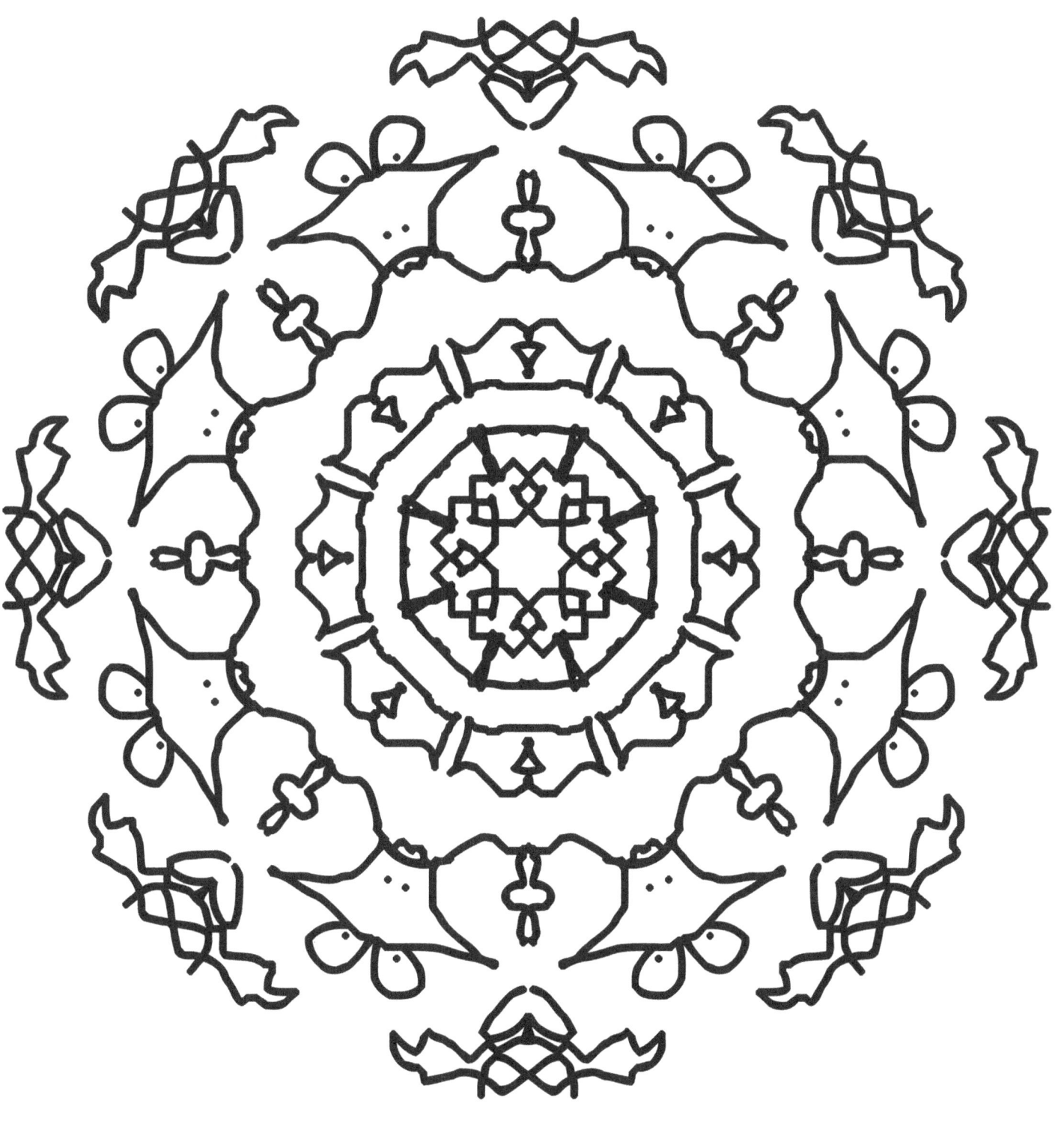

Illustrated by #cherylcolors
www.facebook.com/cherylcolors

Colored by: _____

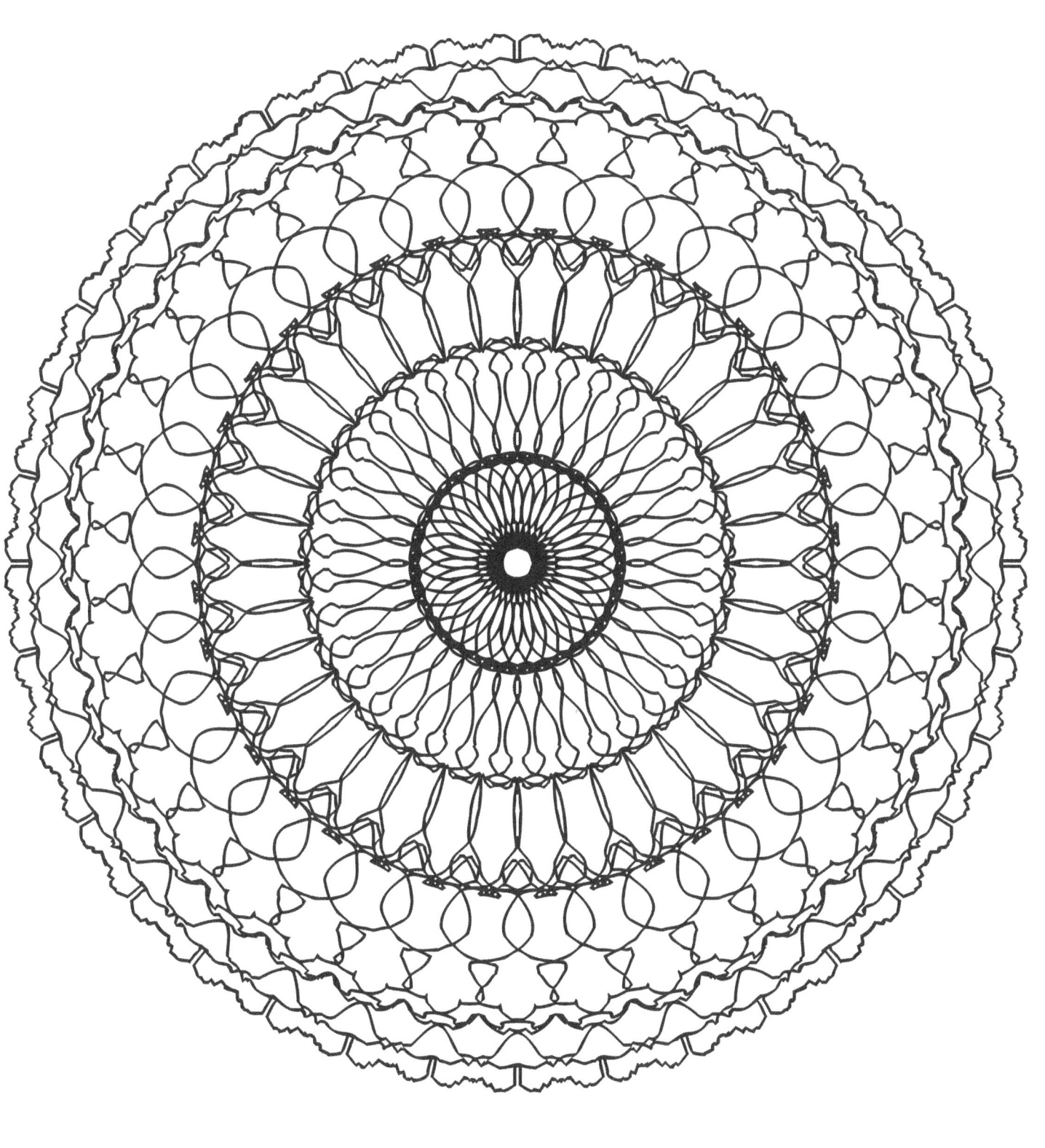

Illustrated by #cherylcolors
www.facebook.com/cherylcolors

Colored by: _____

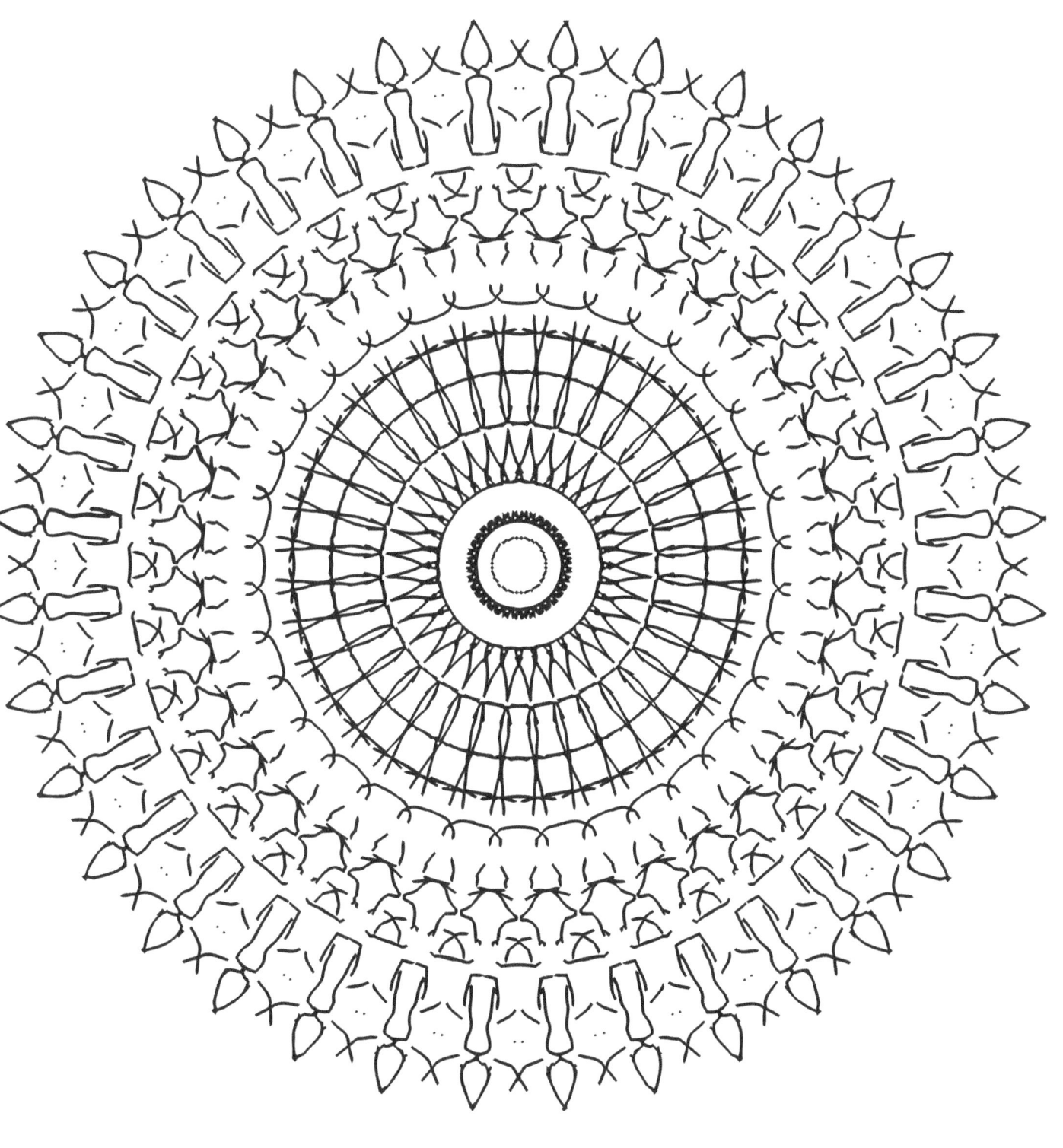

Illustrated by #cherylcolors
www.facebook.com/cherylcolors

Colored by: _____

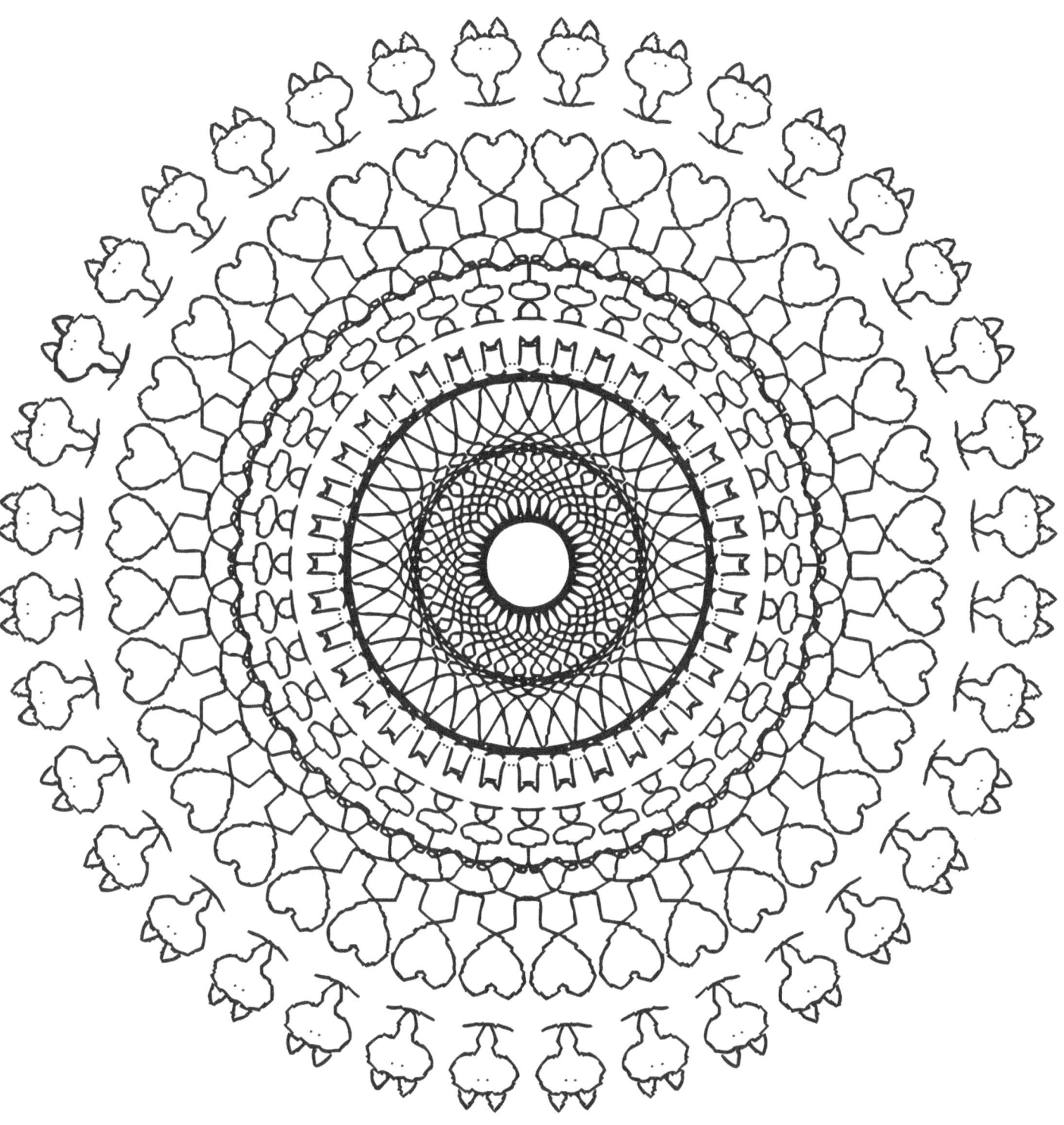

Illustrated by #cherylcolors
www.facebook.com/cherylcolors

Colored by: _____

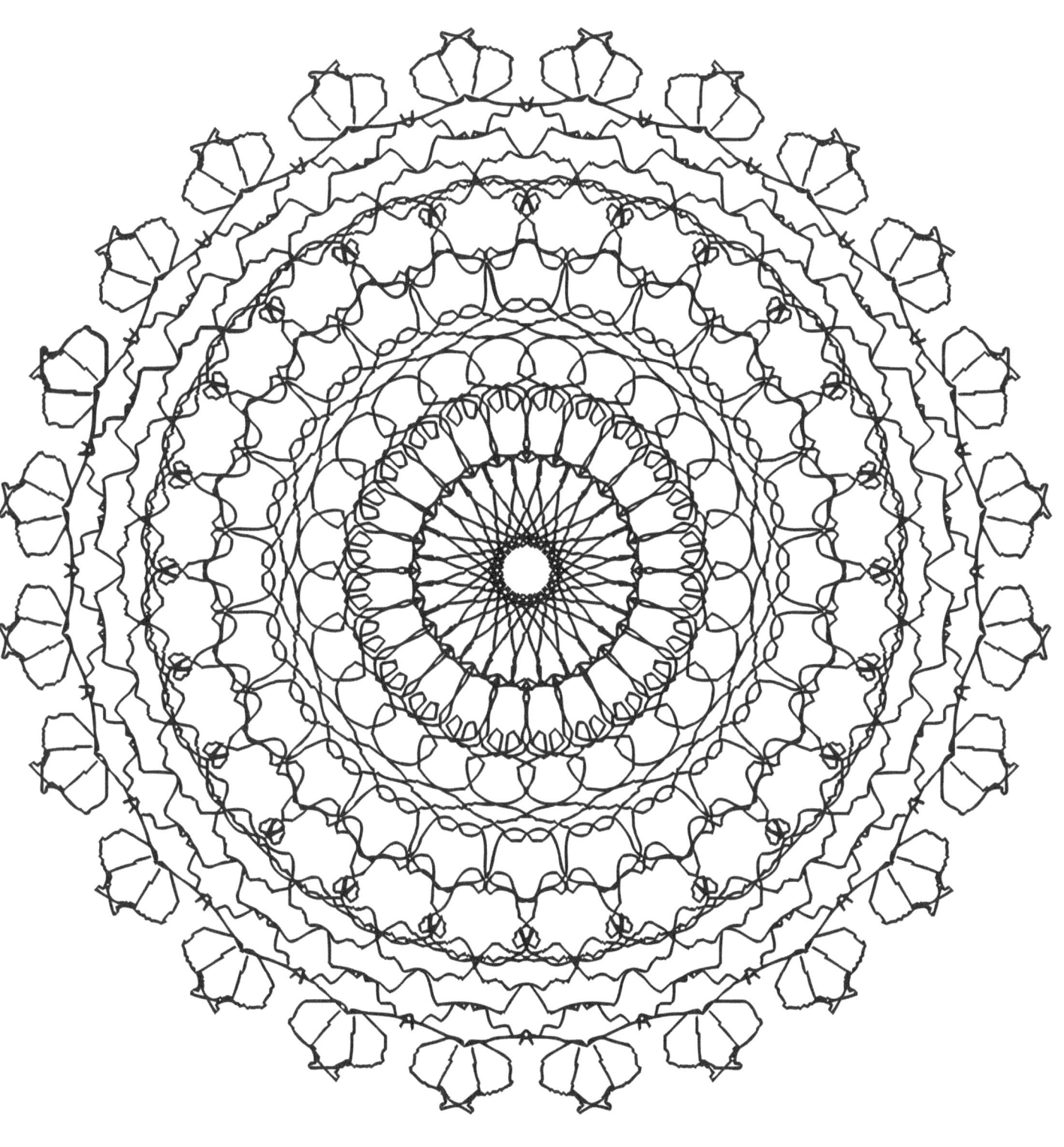

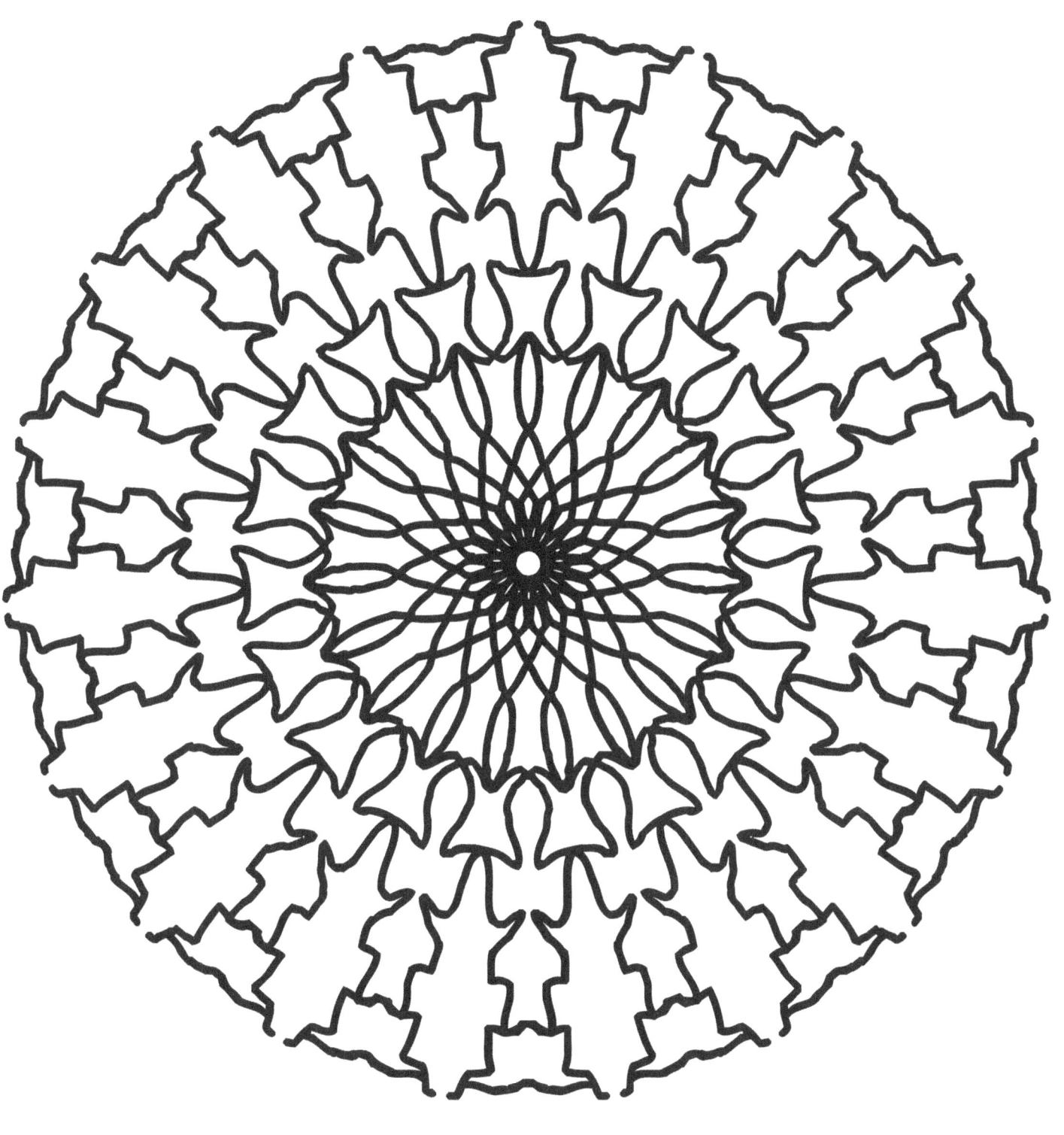

Illustrated by #cherylcolors
www.facebook.com/cherylcolors

Colored by: _____

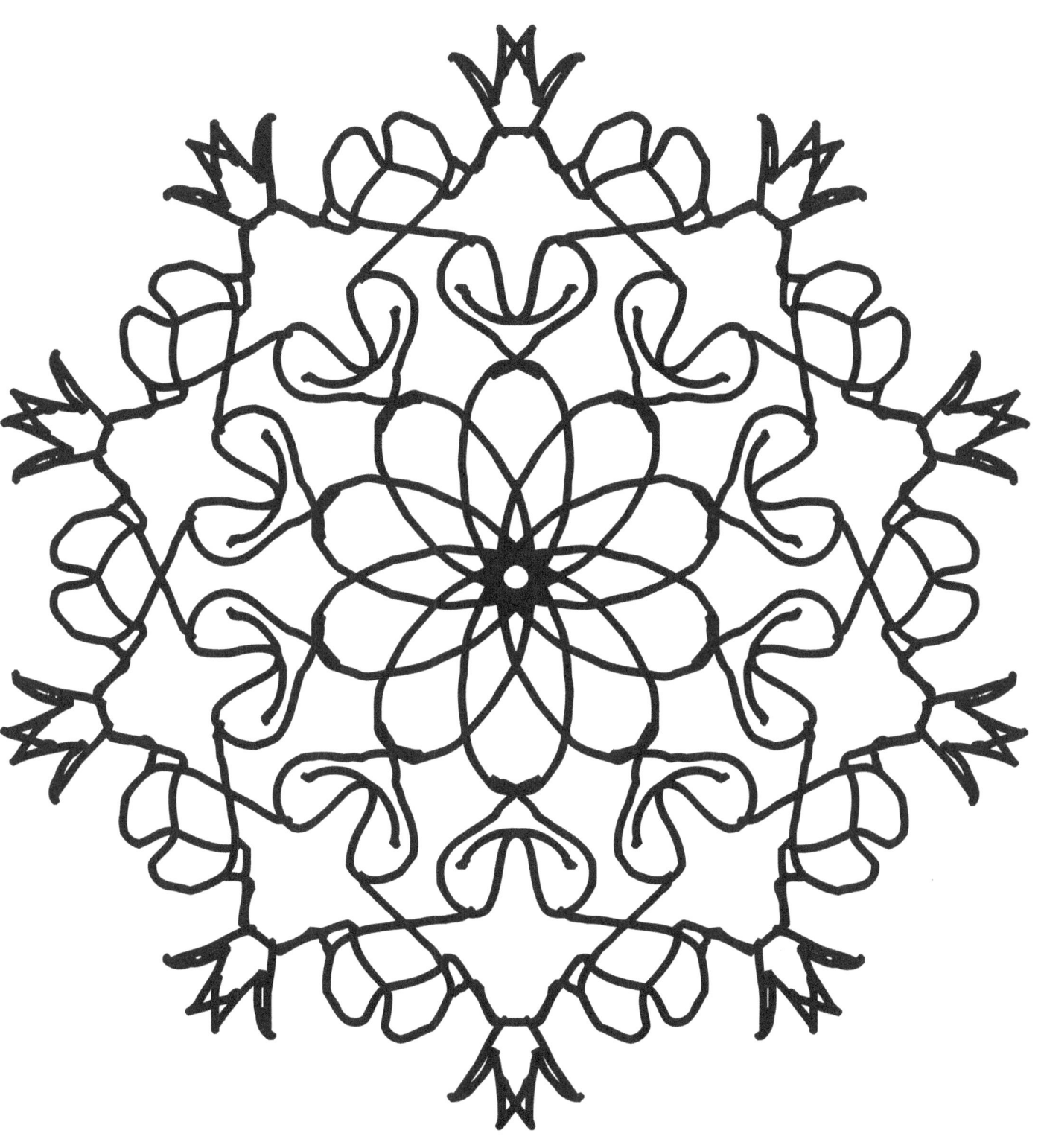

Illustrated by #cherylcolors
www.facebook.com/cherylcolors

Colored by: _____

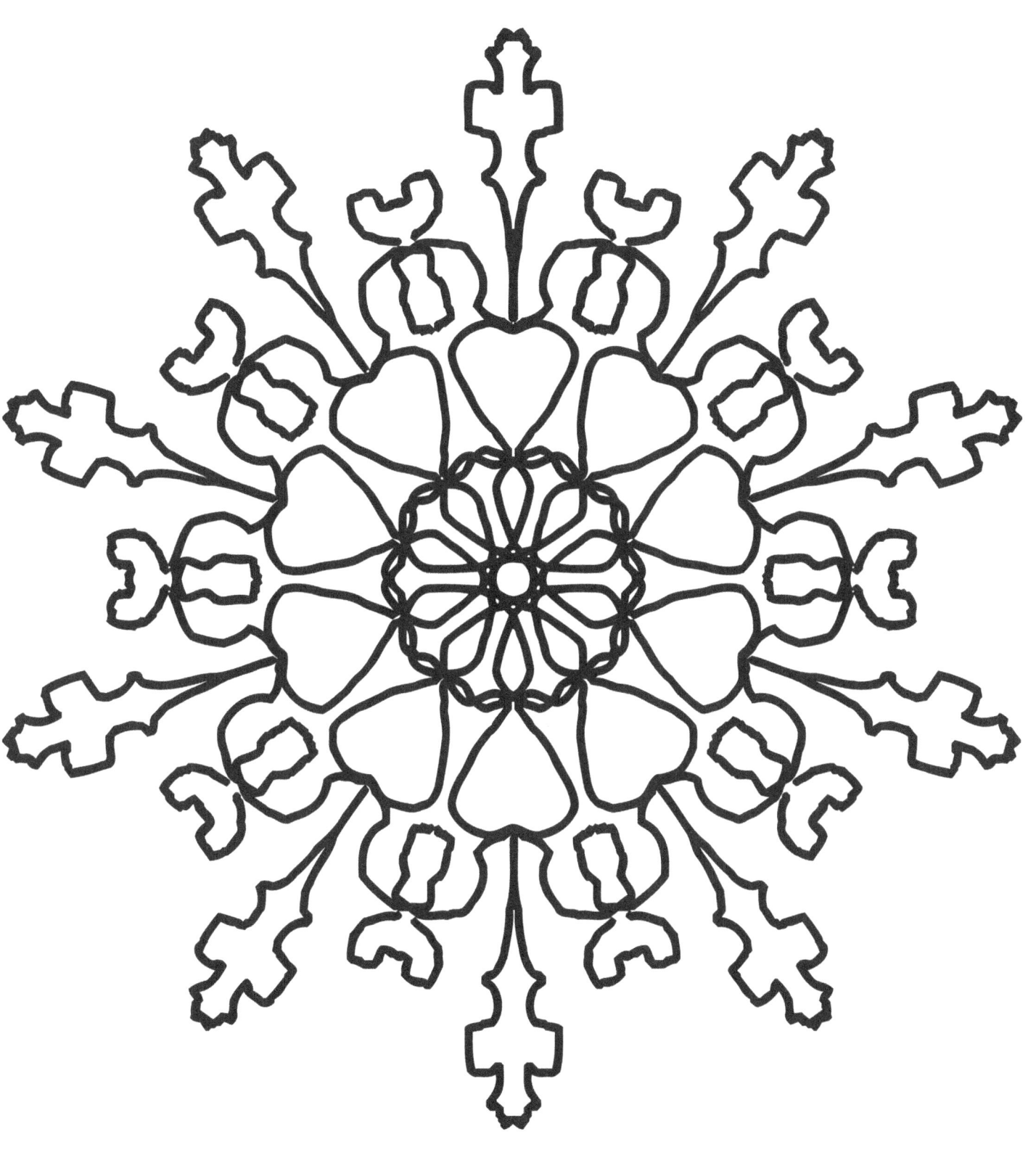

Illustrated by #cherylcolors
www.facebook.com/cherylcolors

Colored by: _____

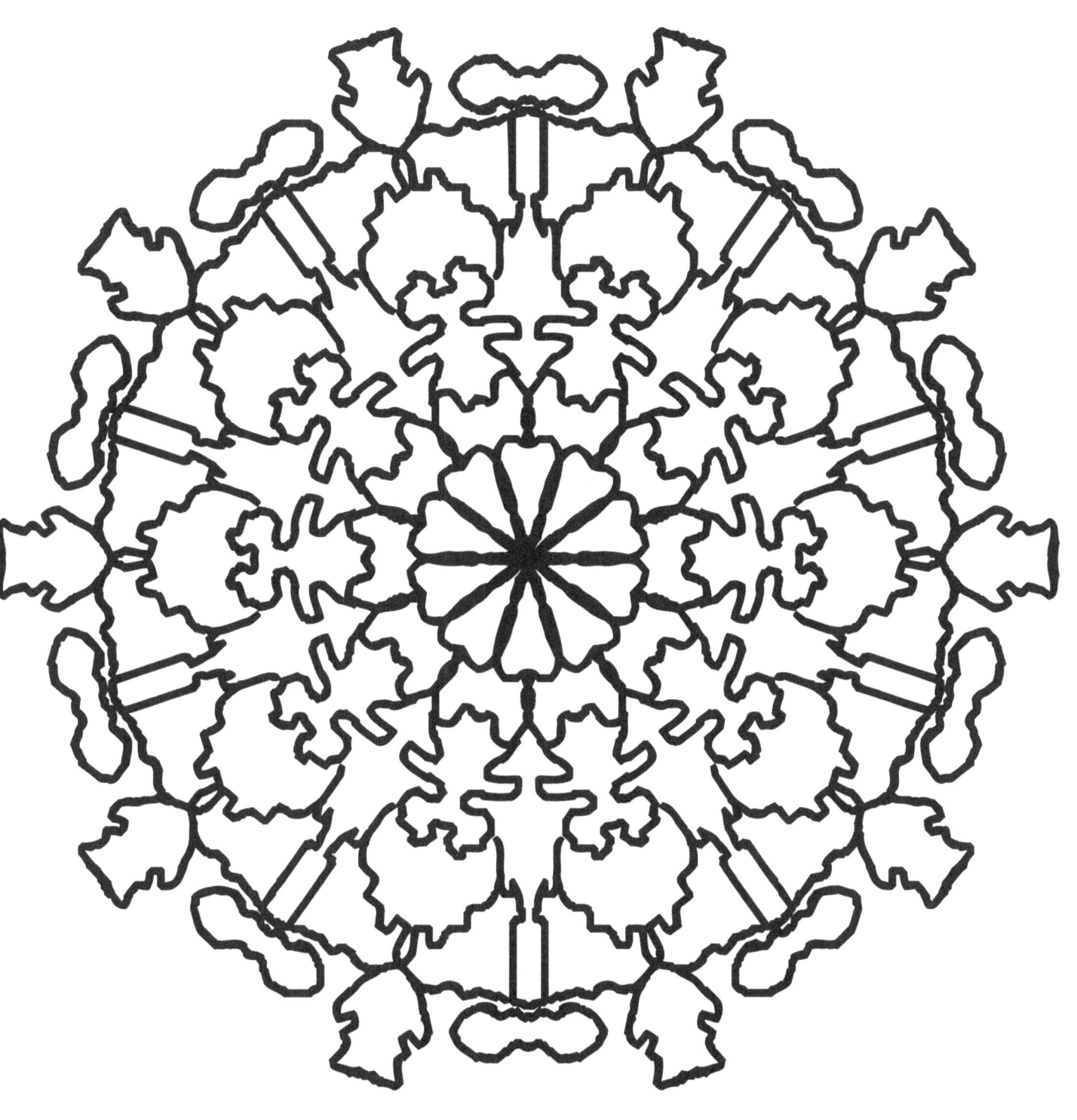

Illustrated by #cherylcolors
www.facebook.com/cherylcolors

Colored by: _____

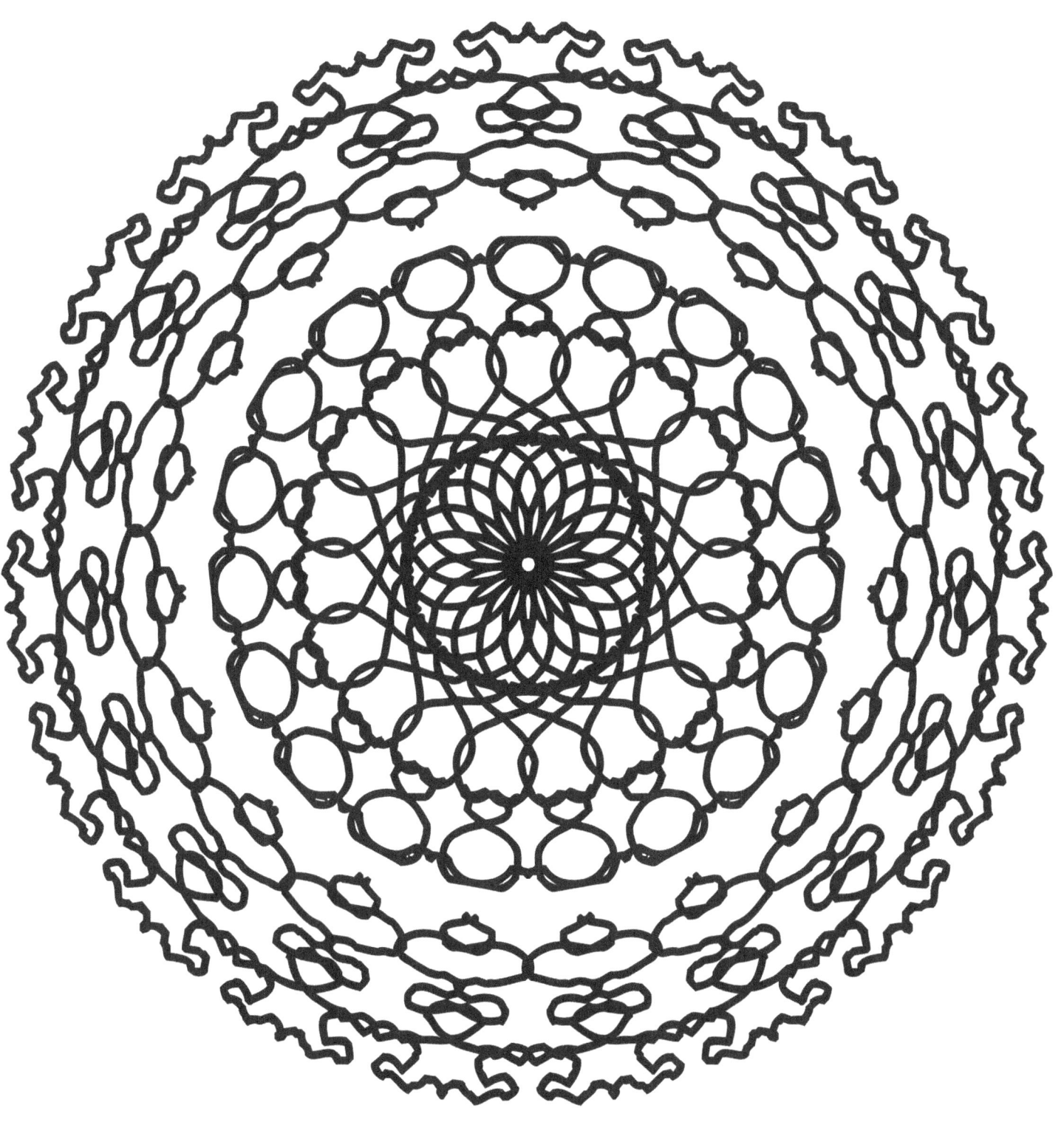

Illustrated by #cherylcolors
www.facebook.com/cherylcolors

Colored by: _____

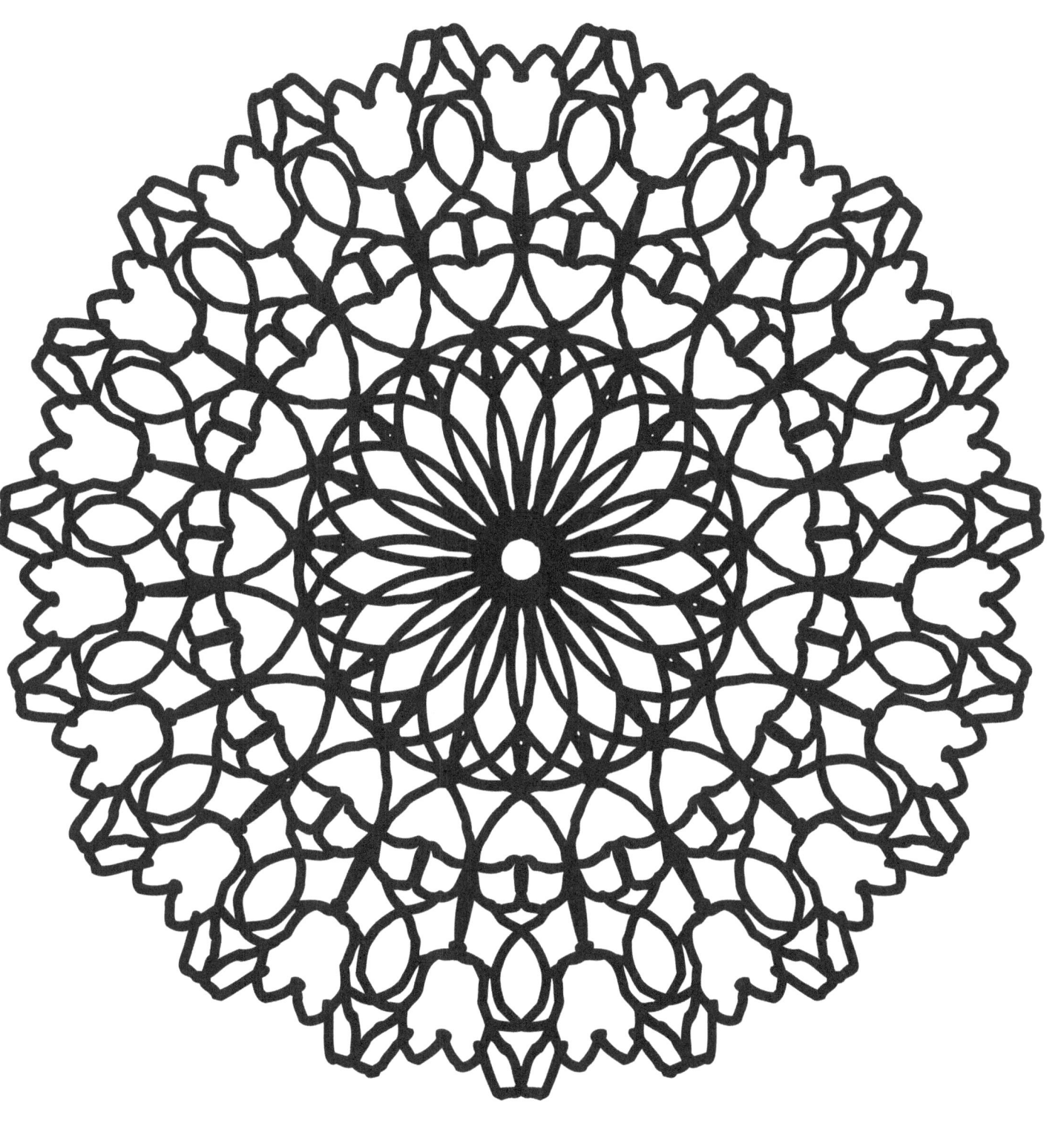

Illustrated by #cherylcolors
www.facebook.com/cherylcolors

Colored by: _____

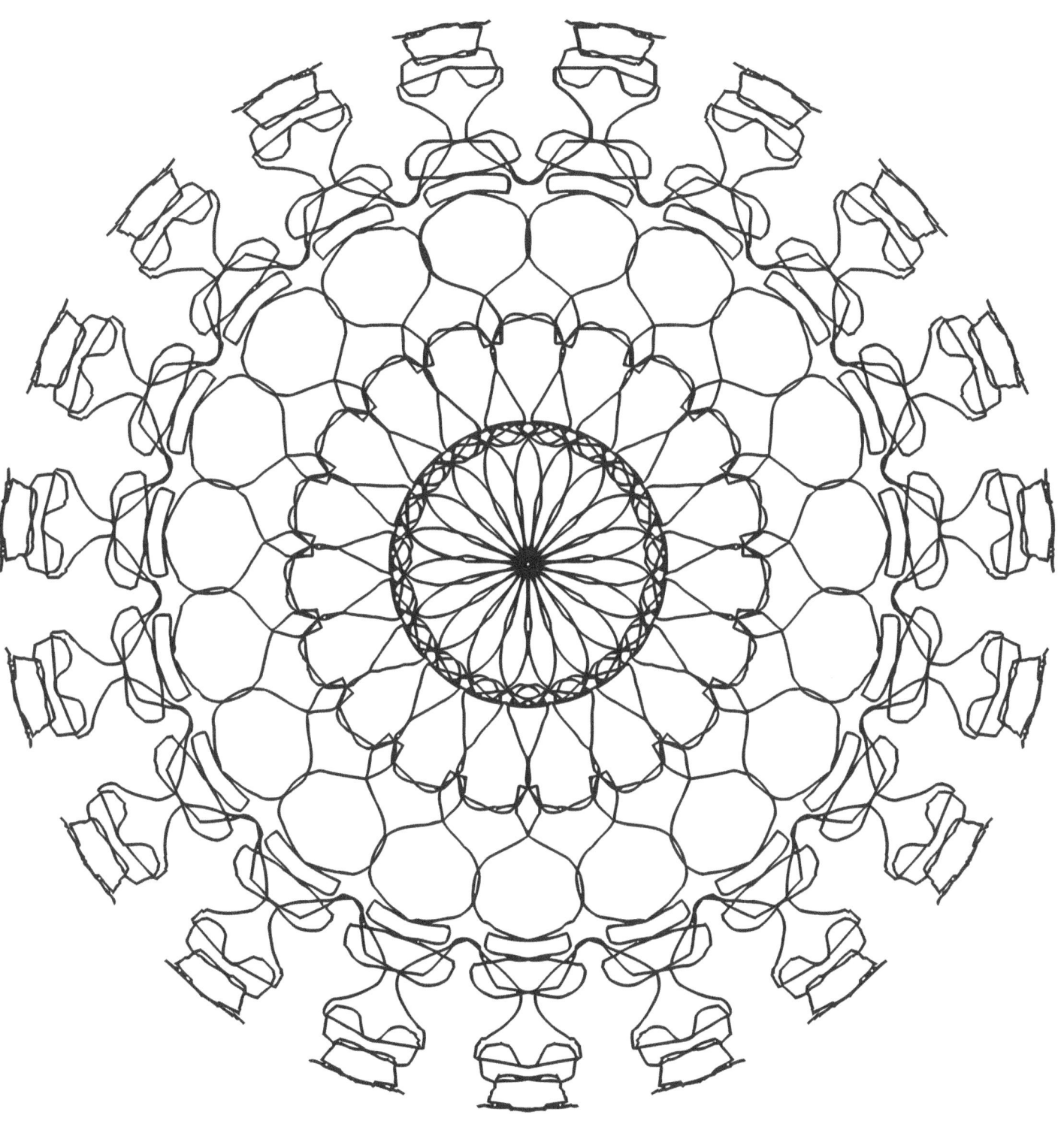

Illustrated by #cherylcolors
www.facebook.com/cherylcolors

Colored by: _____

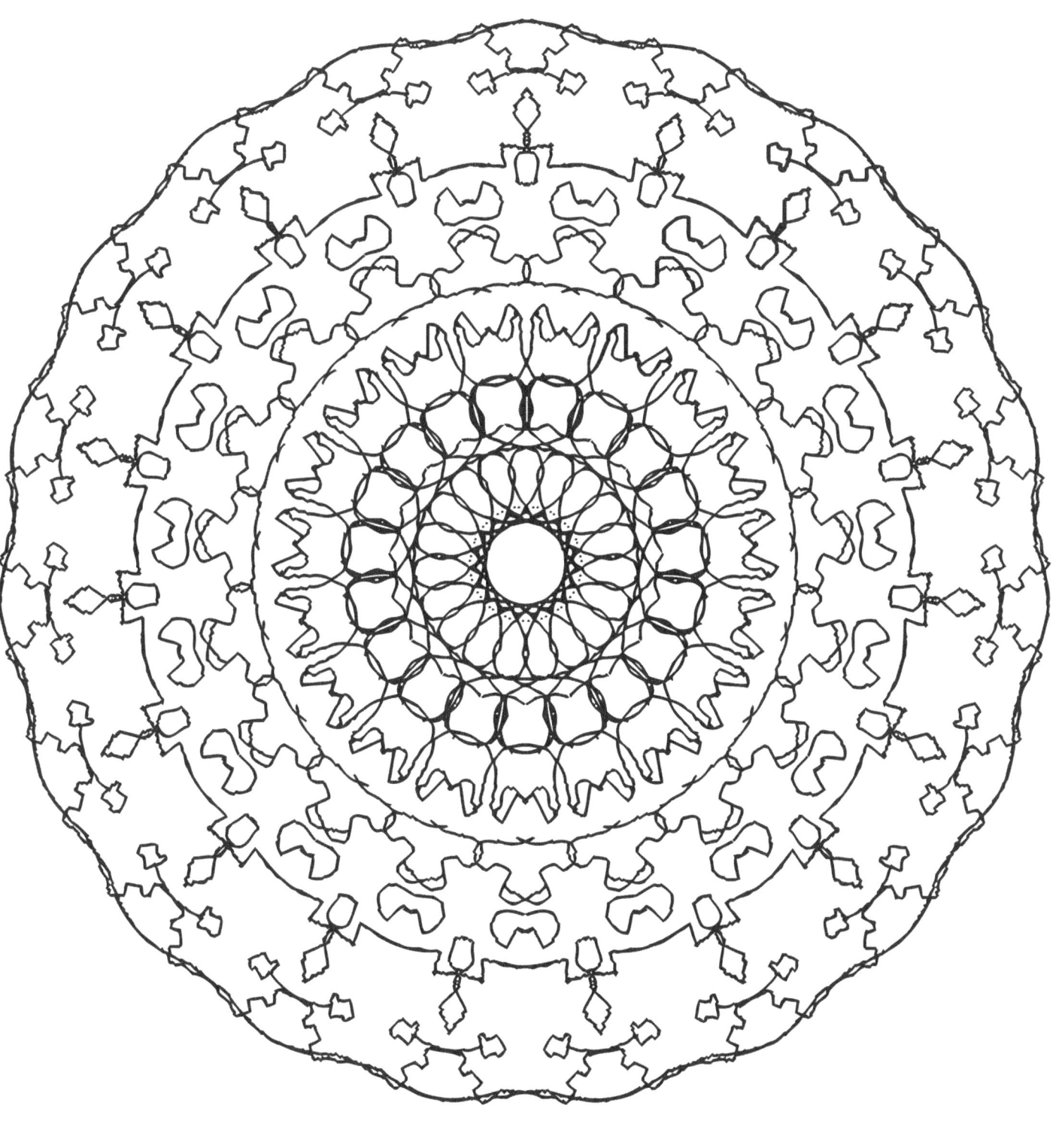

Illustrated by #cherylcolors
www.facebook.com/cherylcolors

Colored by: _____

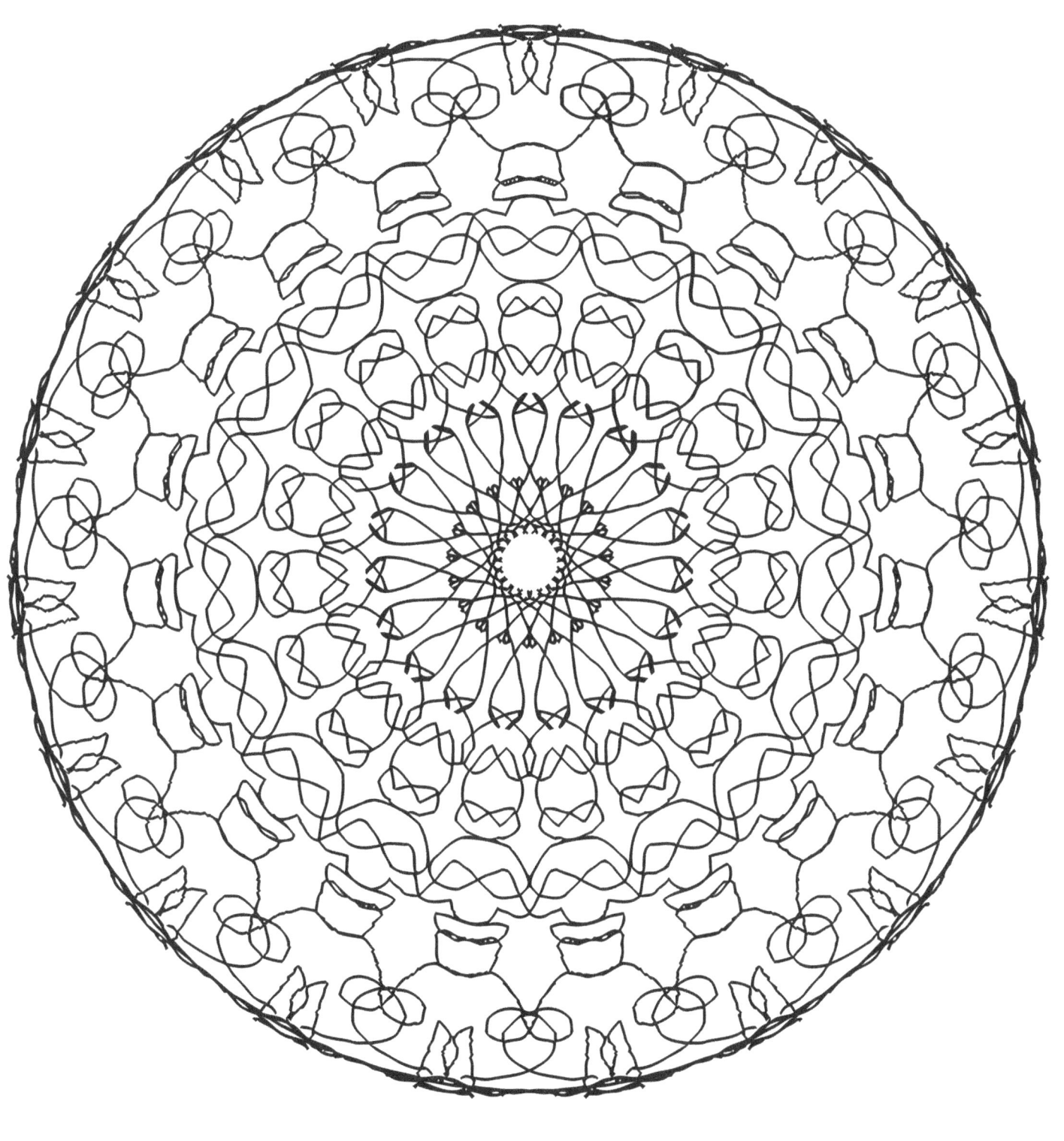

Illustrated by #cherylcolors
www.facebook.com/cherylcolors

Colored by: _____

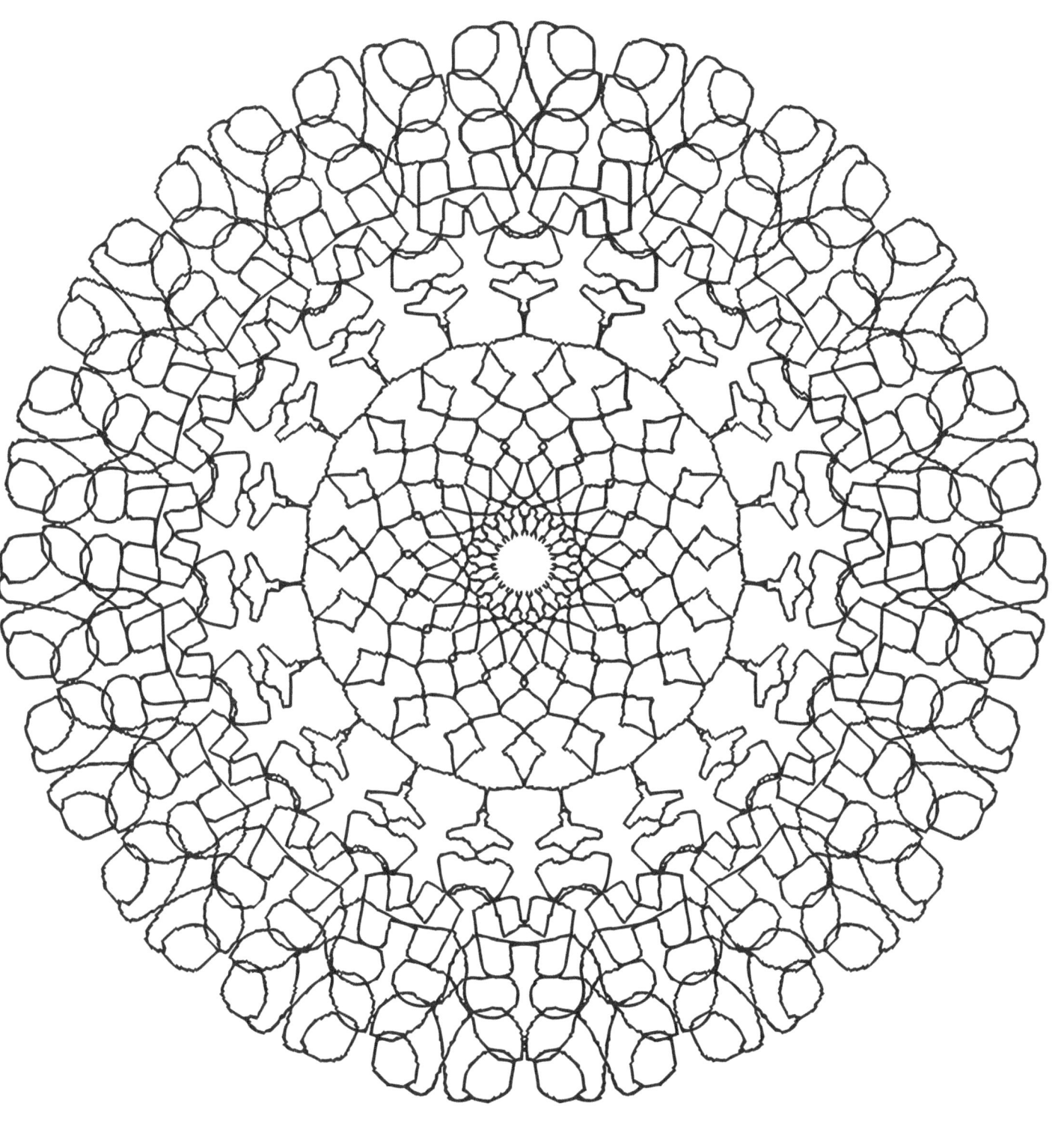

Illustrated by #cherylcolors
www.facebook.com/cherylcolors

Colored by: _____

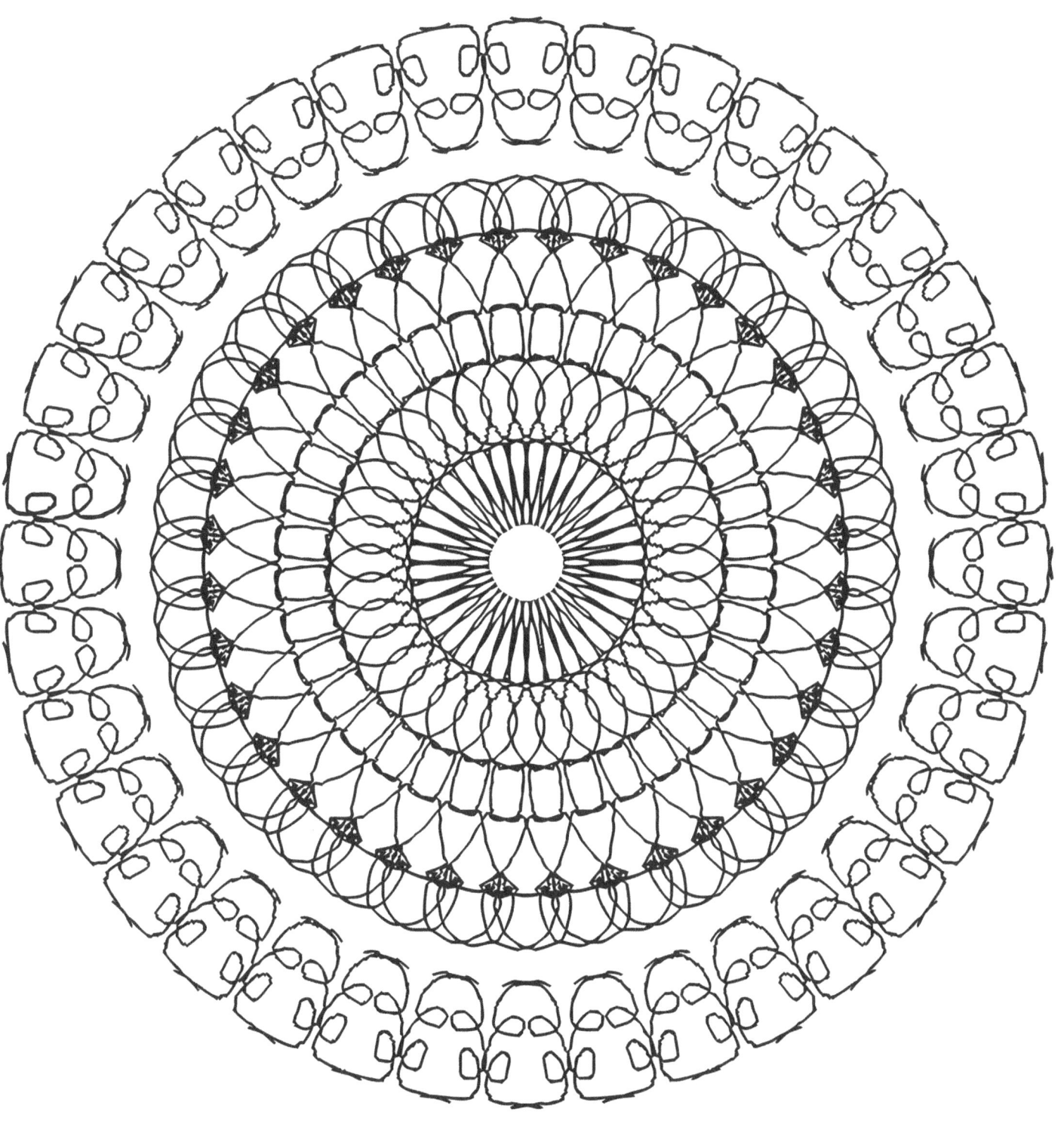

Illustrated by #cherylcolors
www.facebook.com/cherylcolors

Colored by: _____

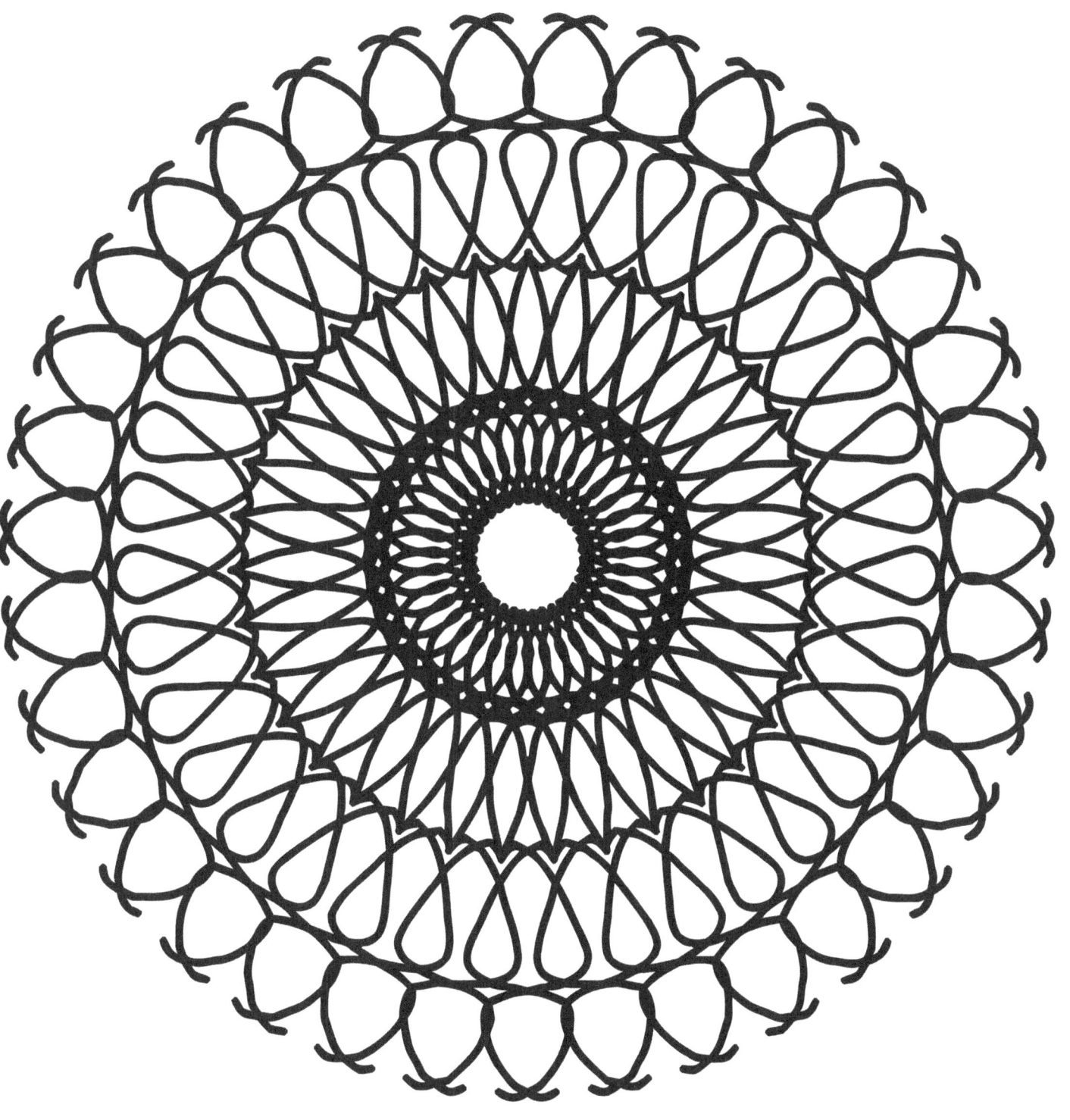

Illustrated by #cherylcolors
www.facebook.com/cherylcolors

Colored by: _____

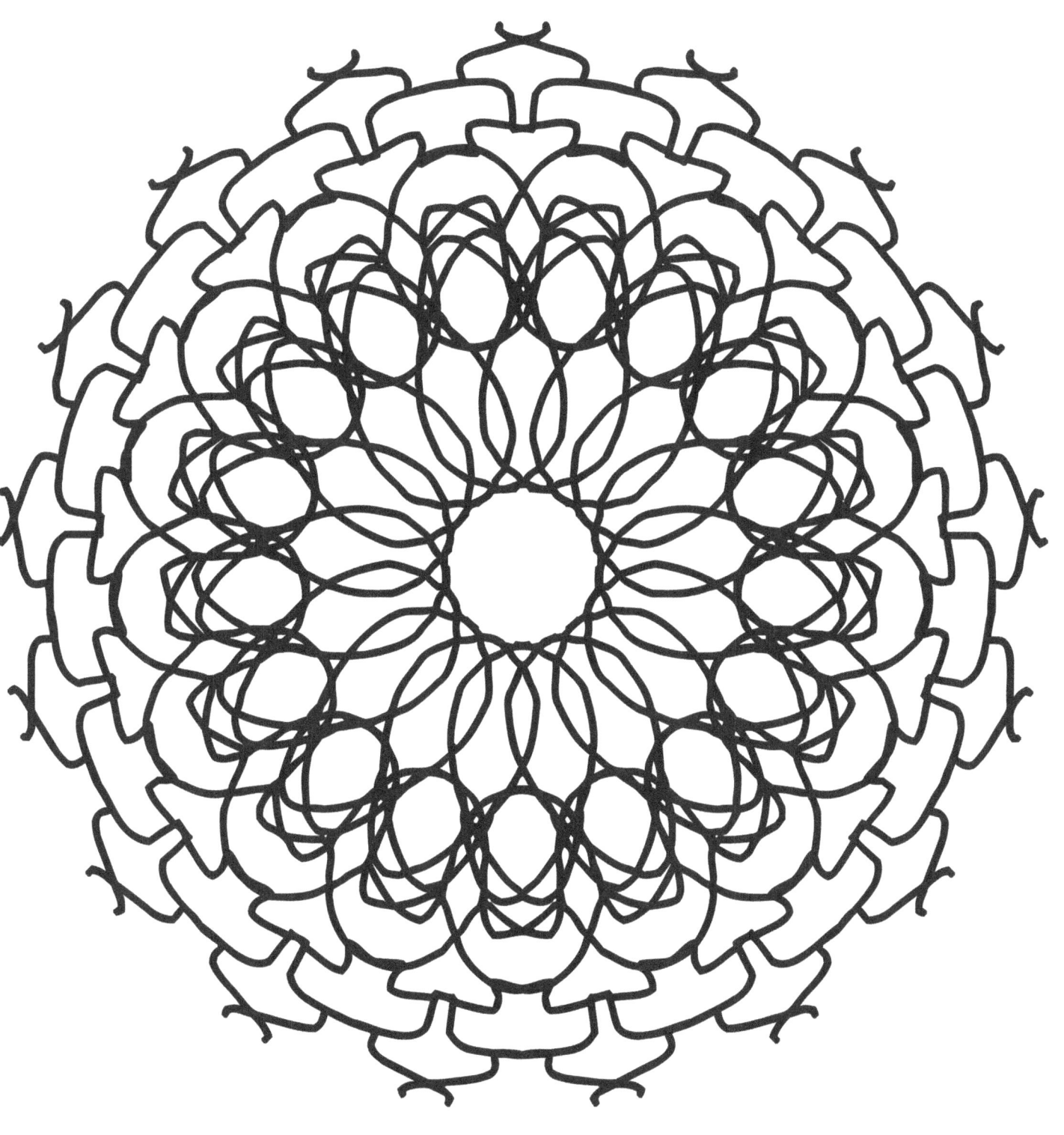

Illustrated by #cherylcolors
www.facebook.com/cherylcolors

Colored by: _____

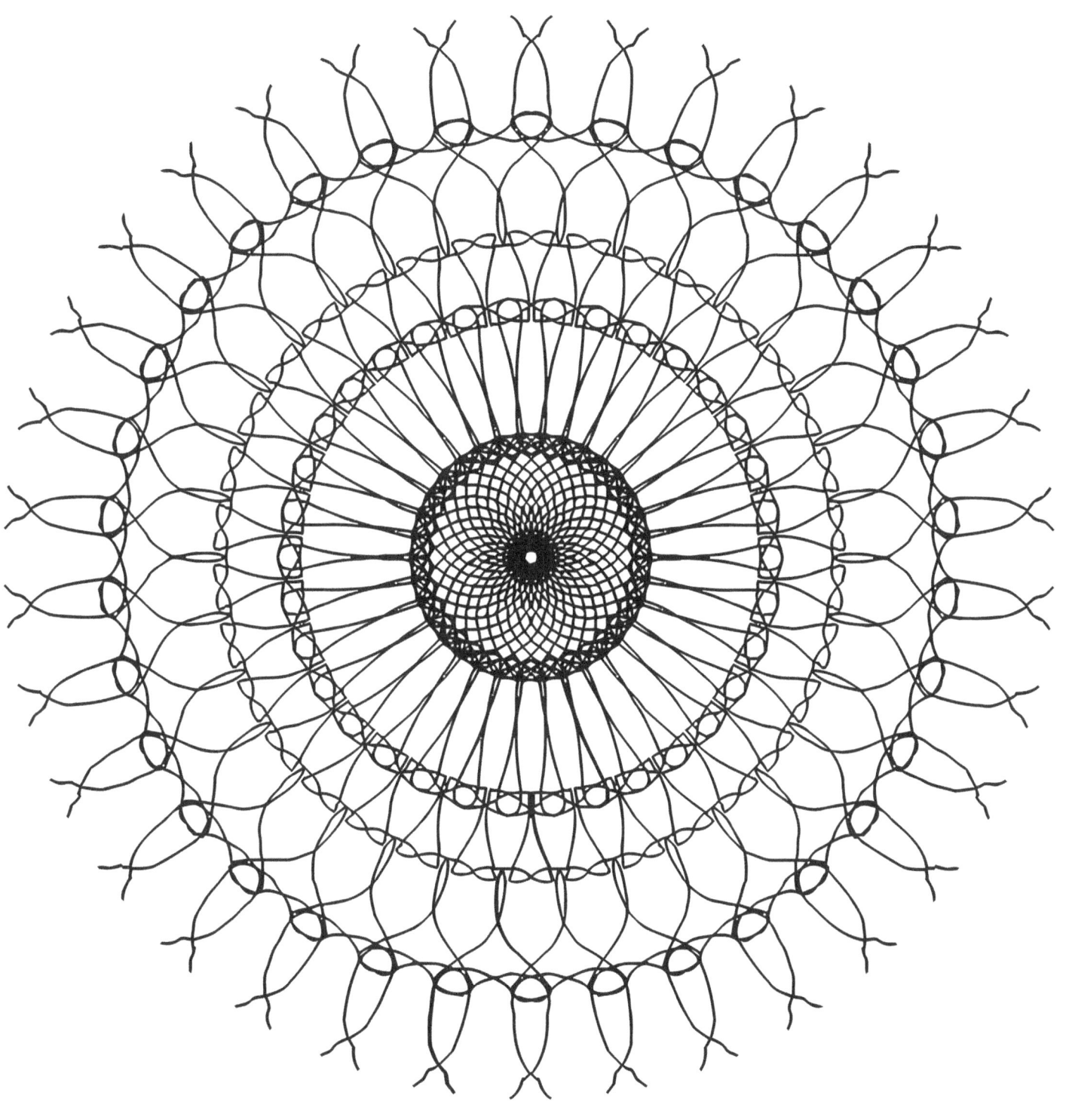

Illustrated by #cherylcolors
www.facebook.com/cherylcolors

Colored by: _____

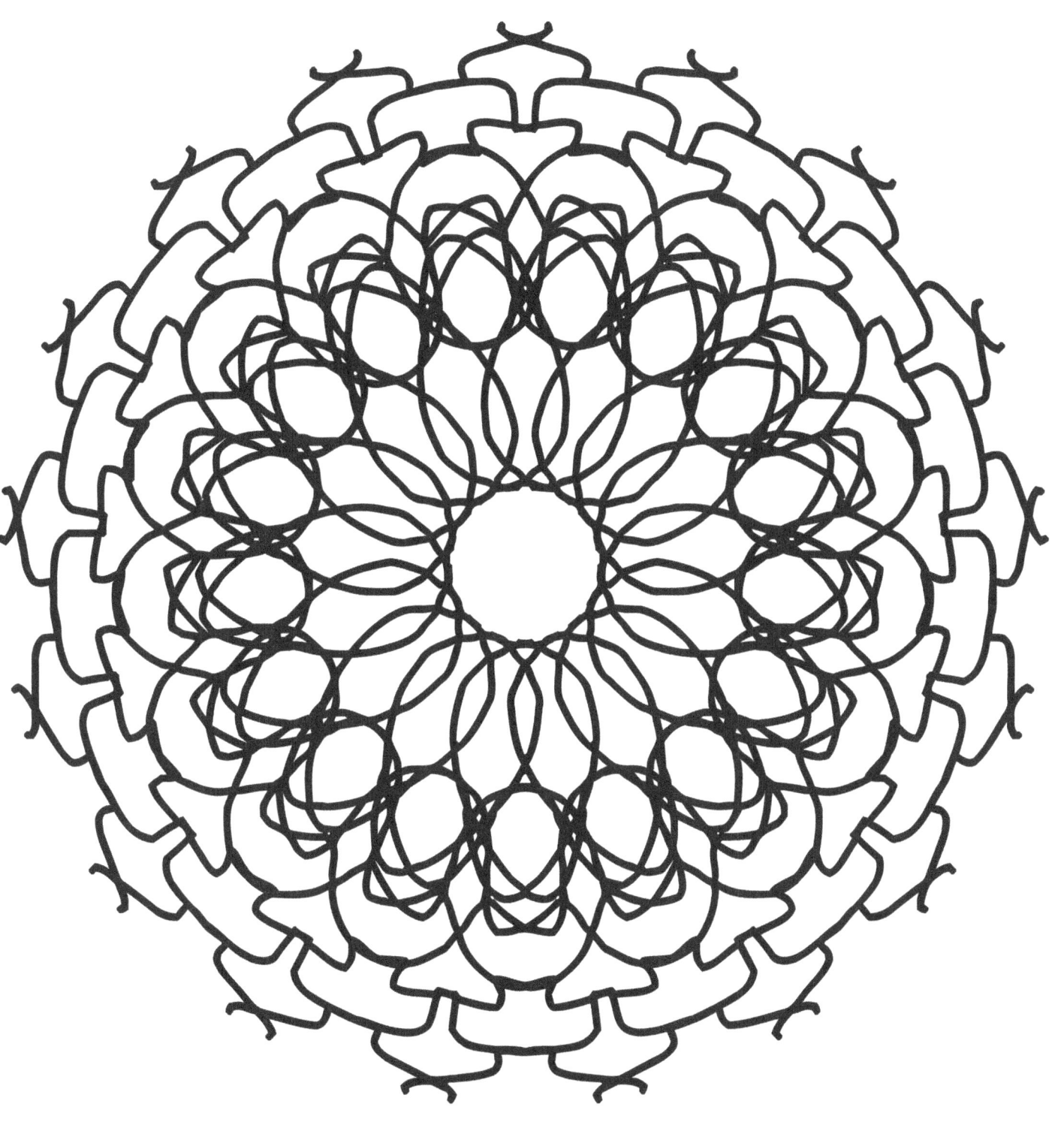

Illustrated by #cherylcolors
www.facebook.com/cherylcolors

Colored by: _____

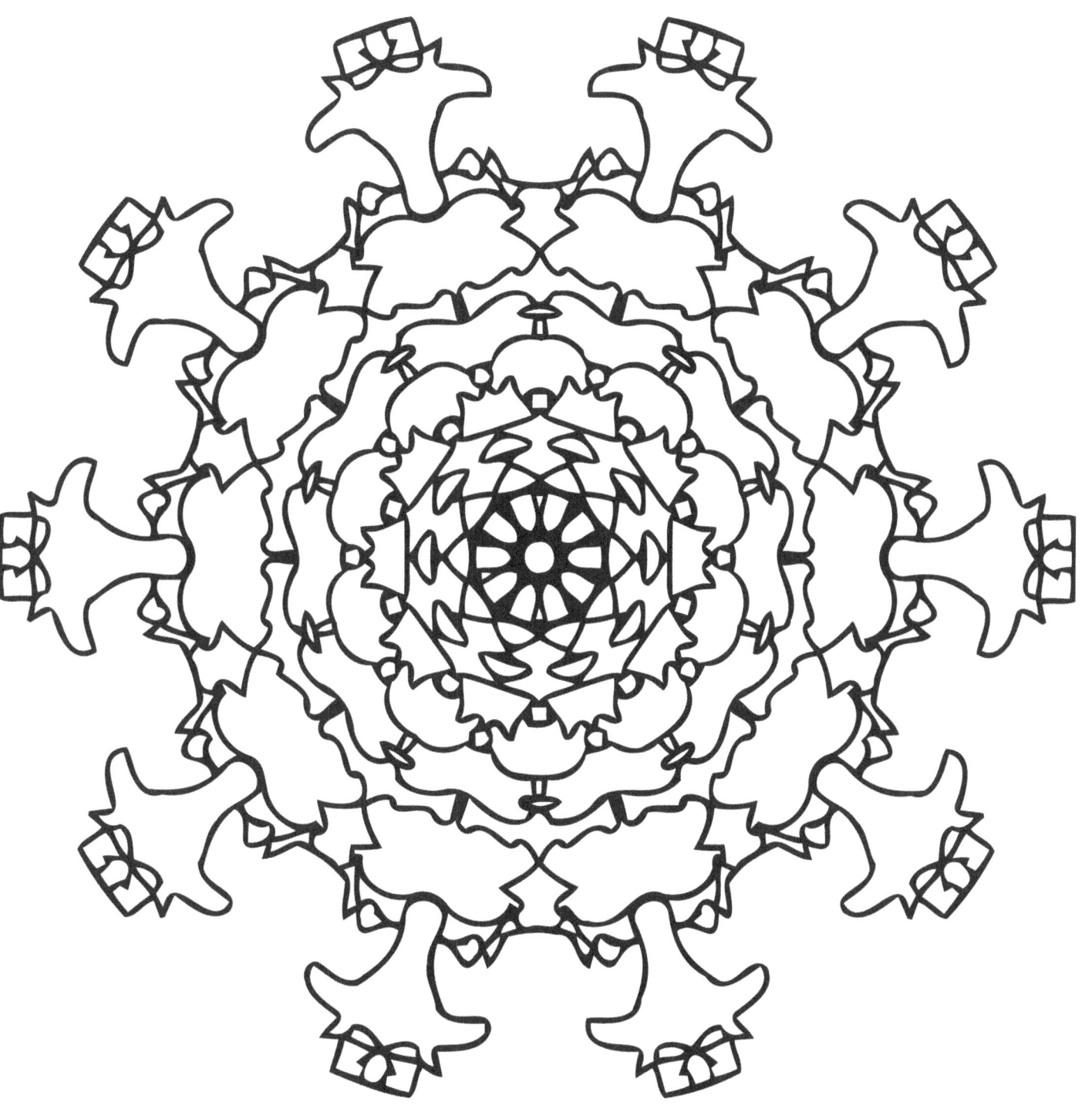

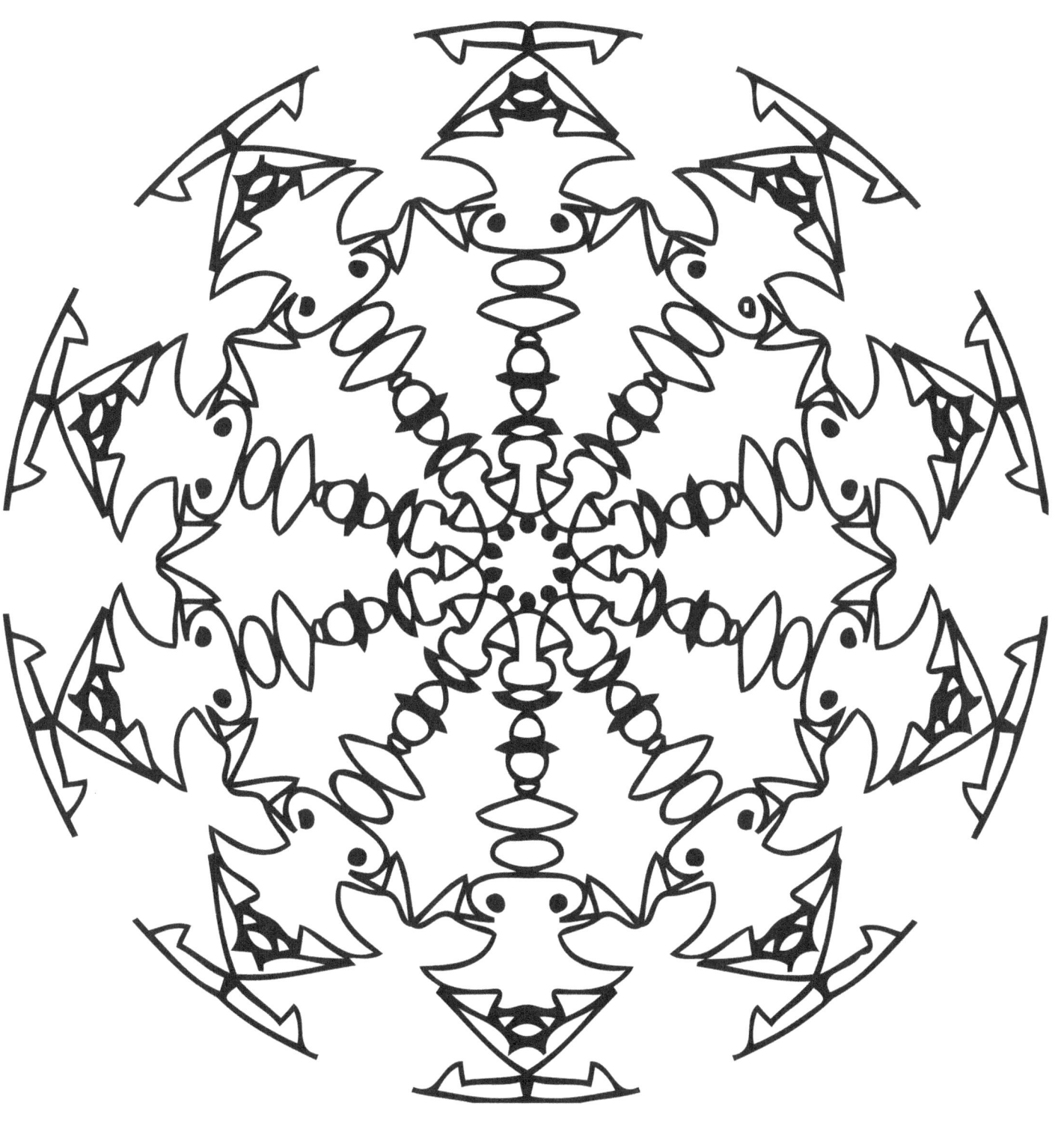

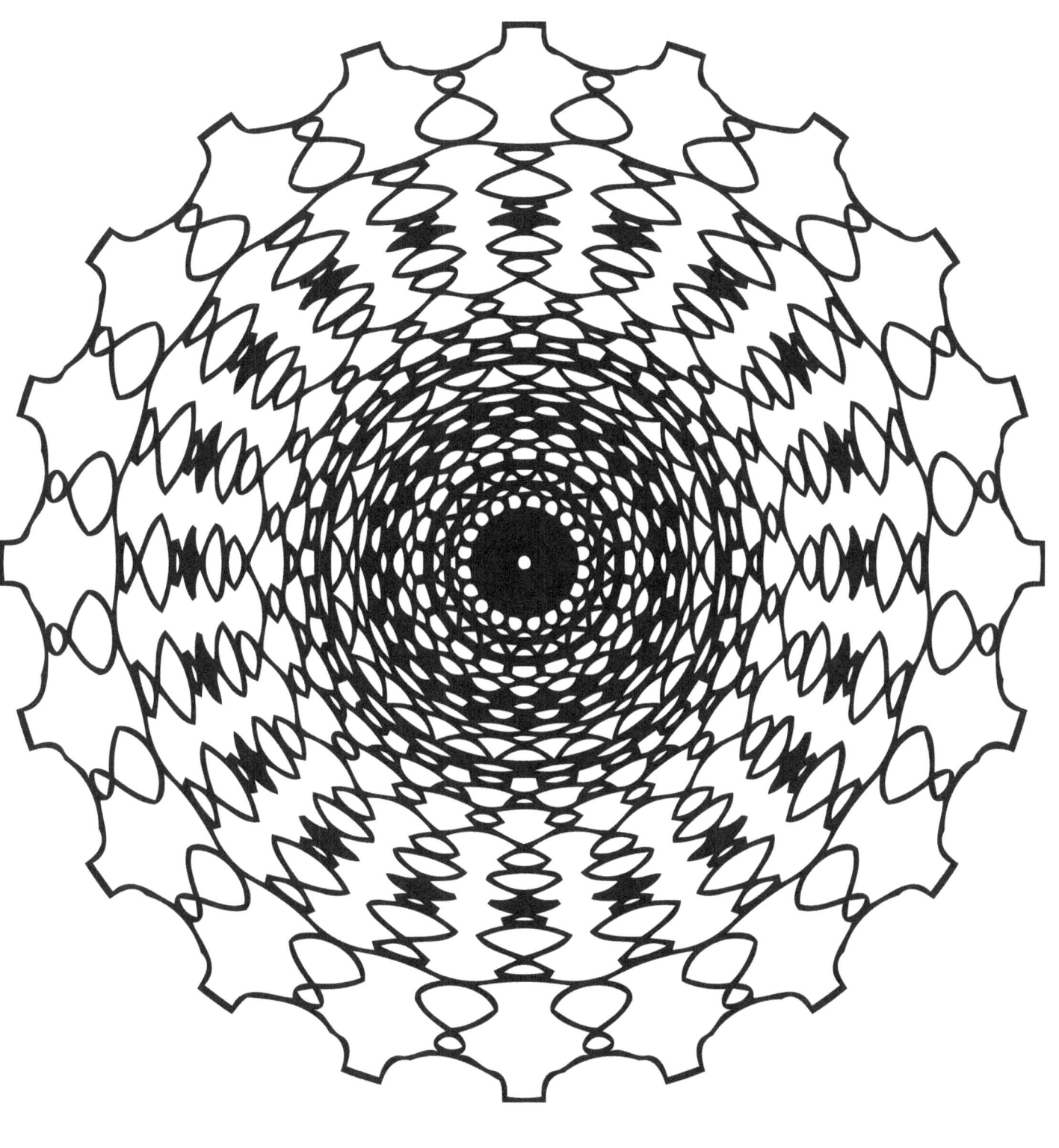

Illustrated by #cherylcolors
www.facebook.com/cherylcolors

Colored by: _____

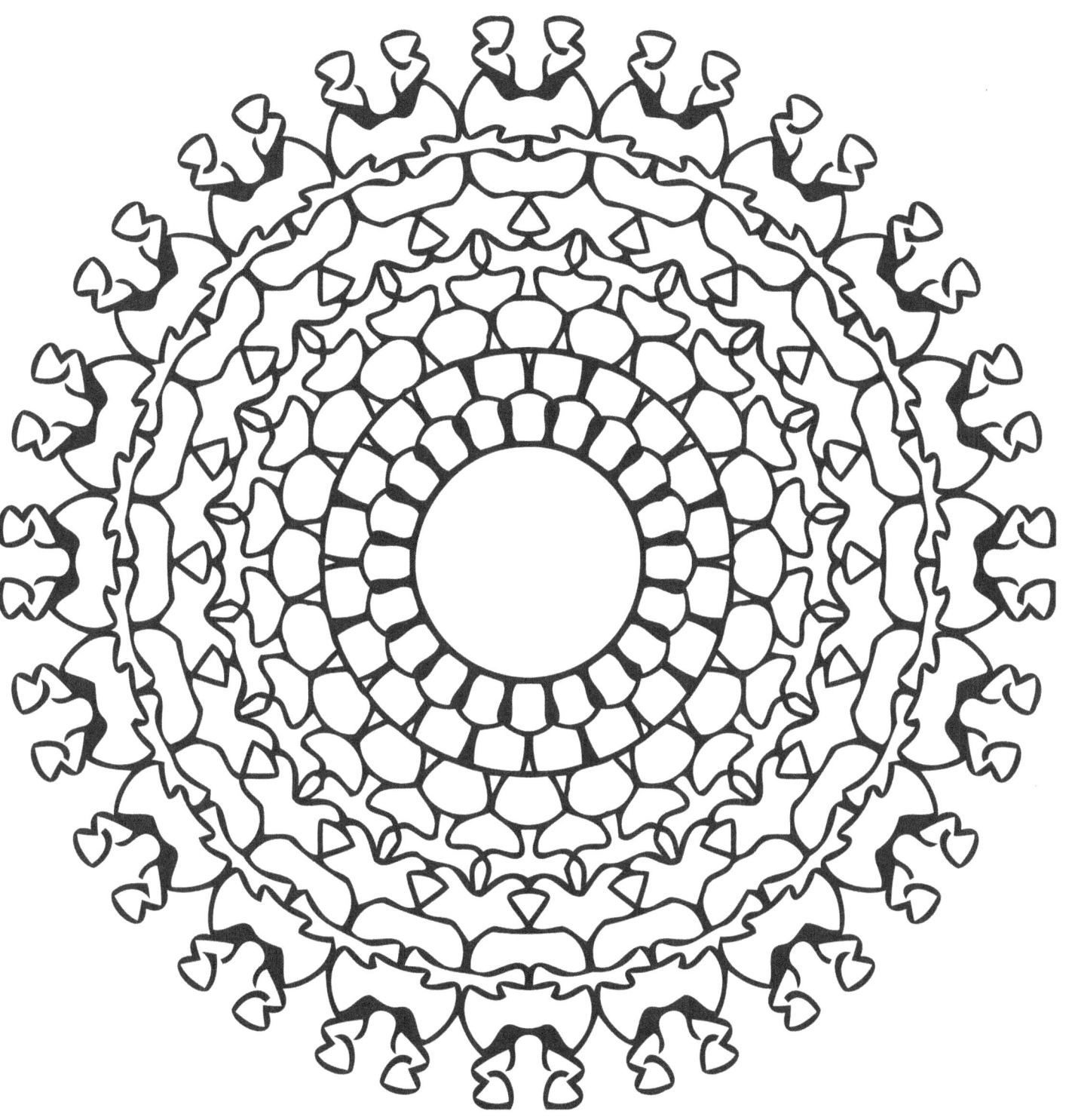

Illustrated by #cherylcolors
www.facebook.com/cherylcolors

Colored by: _____

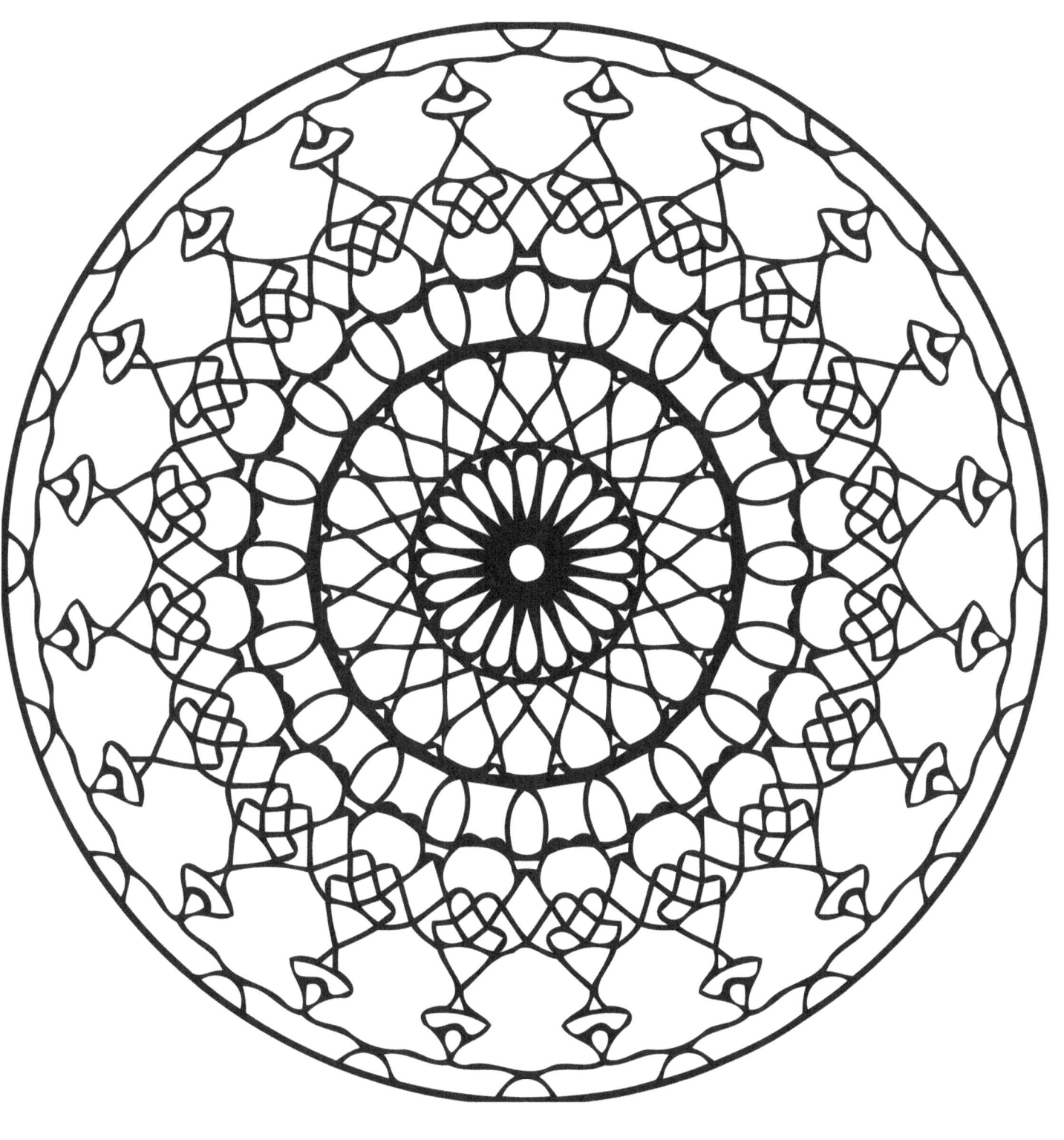

Illustrated by #cherylcolors
www.facebook.com/cherylcolors

Colored by: _____

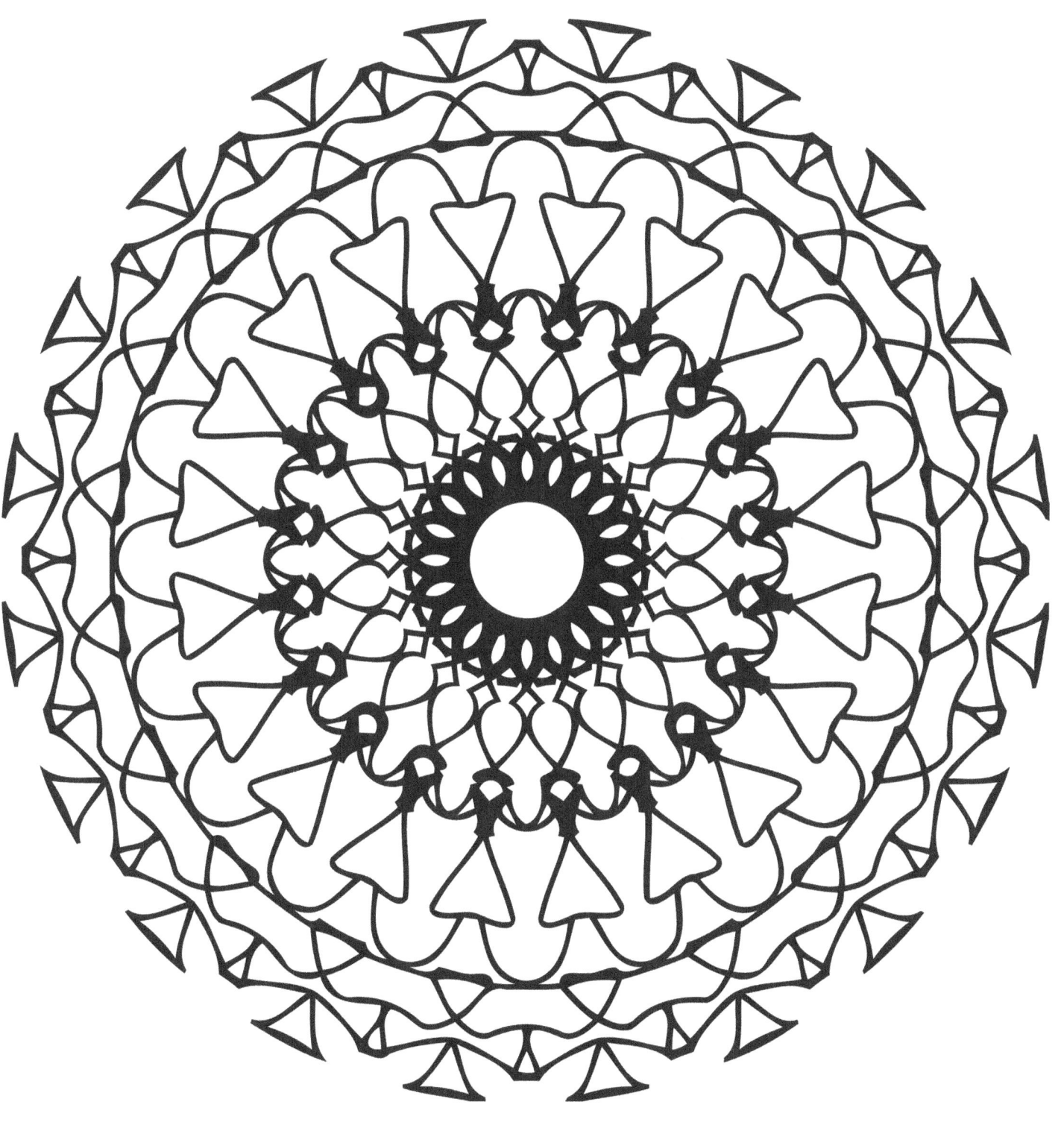

Illustrated by #cherylcolors
www.facebook.com/cherylcolors

Colored by: _____

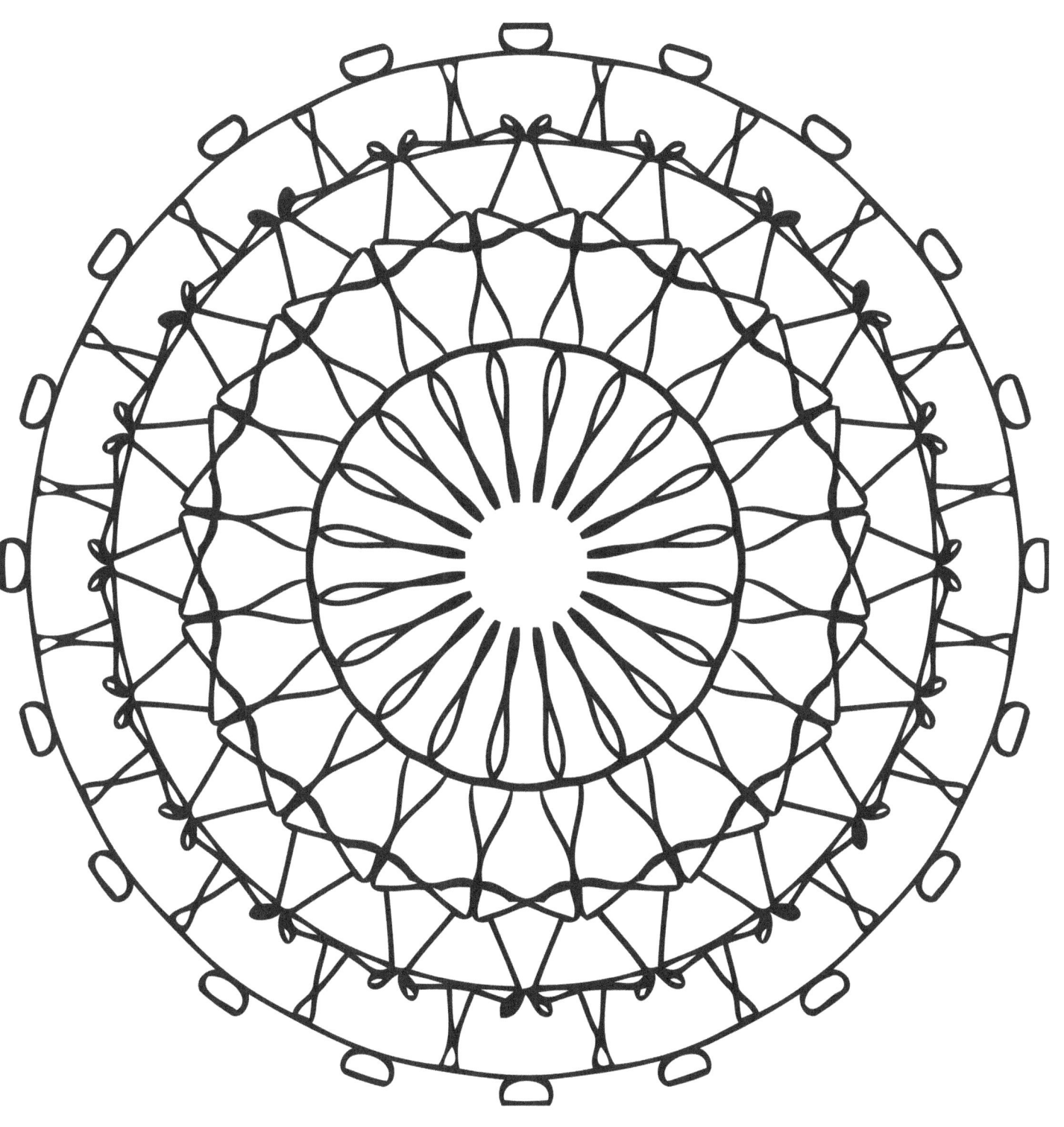

Illustrated by #cherylcolors
www.facebook.com/cherylcolors

Colored by: _____

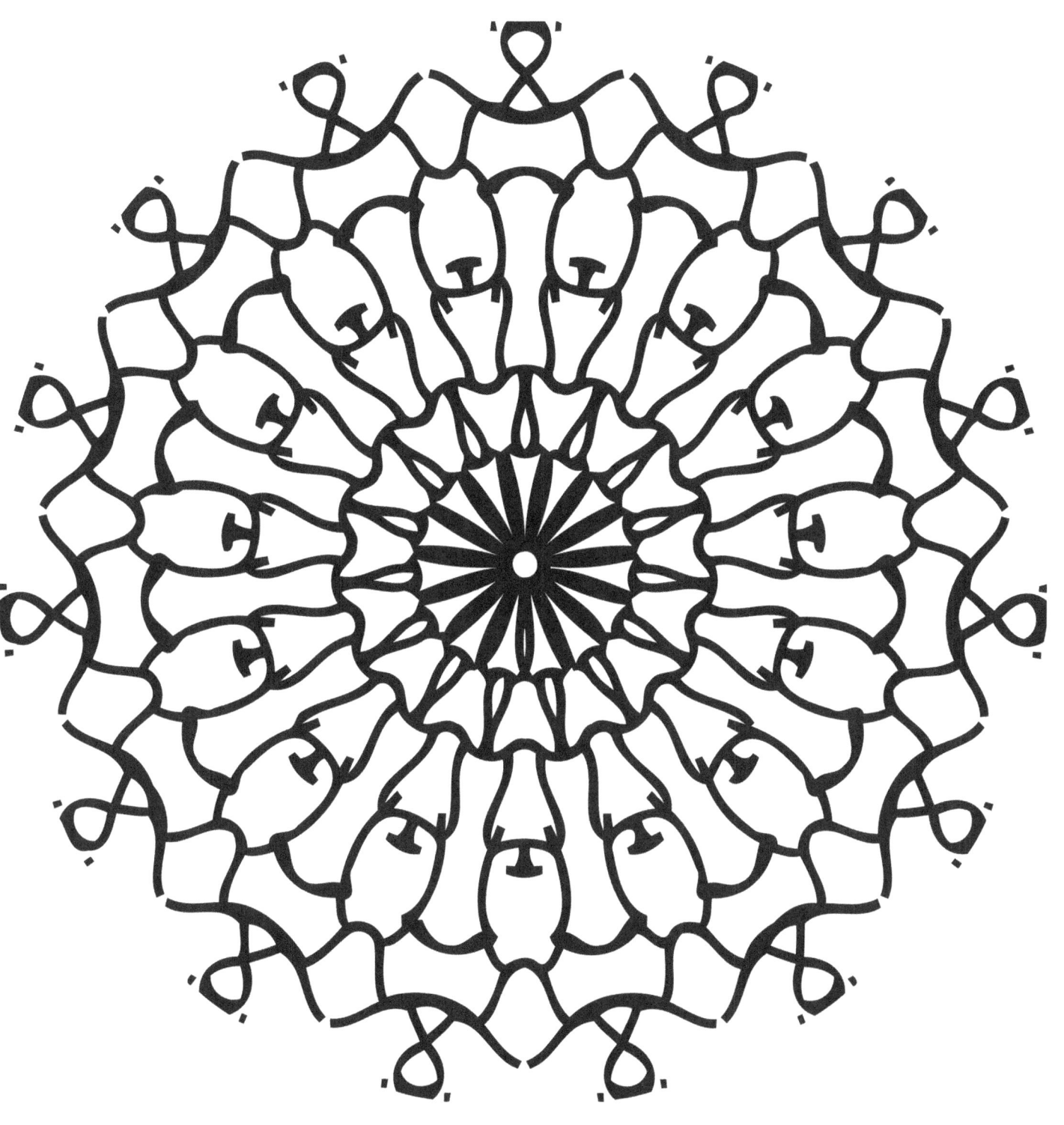

Illustrated by #cherylcolors
www.facebook.com/cherylcolors

Colored by: _____

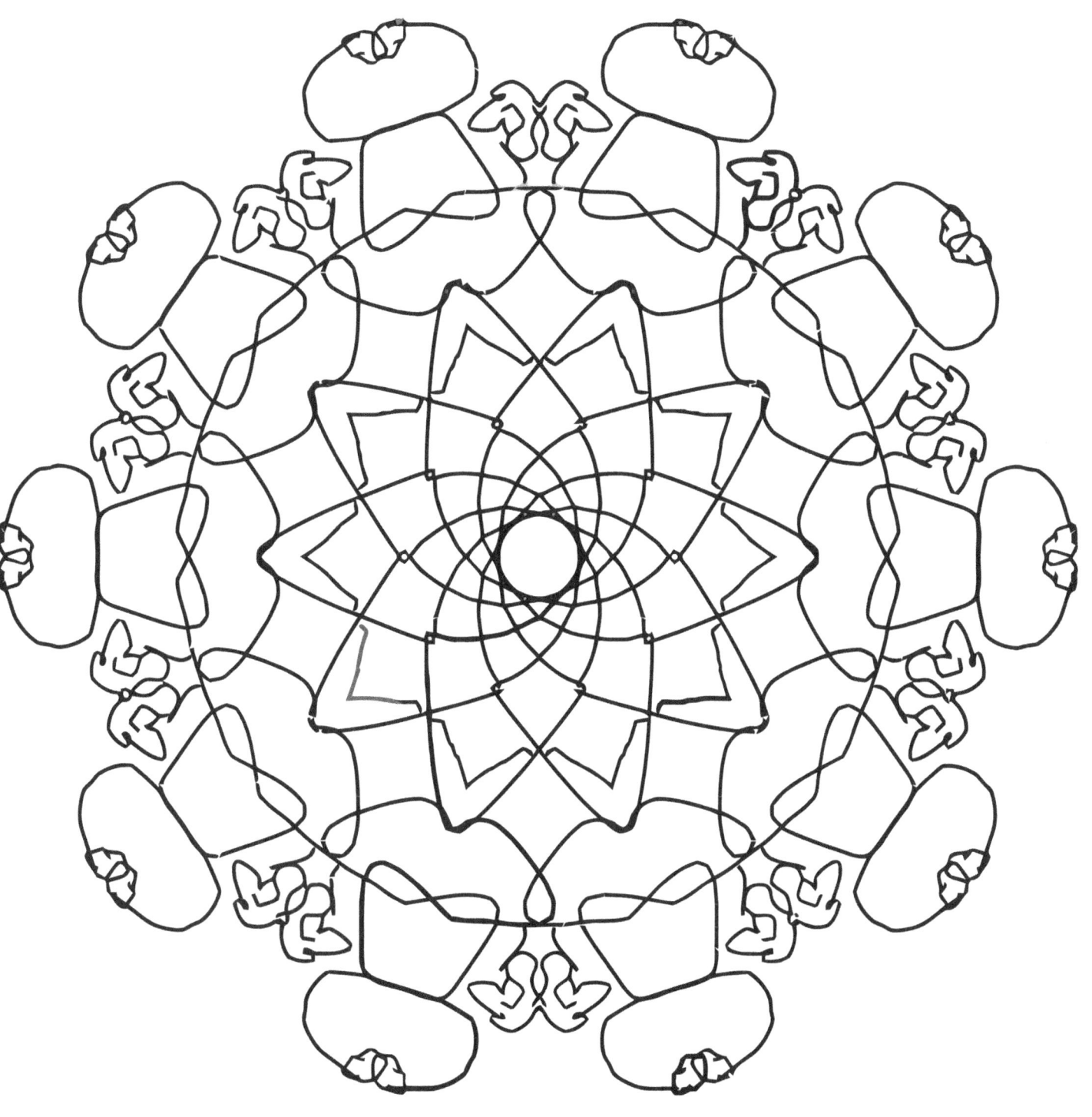

Illustrated by #cherylcolors
www.facebook.com/cherylcolors

Colored by: _____

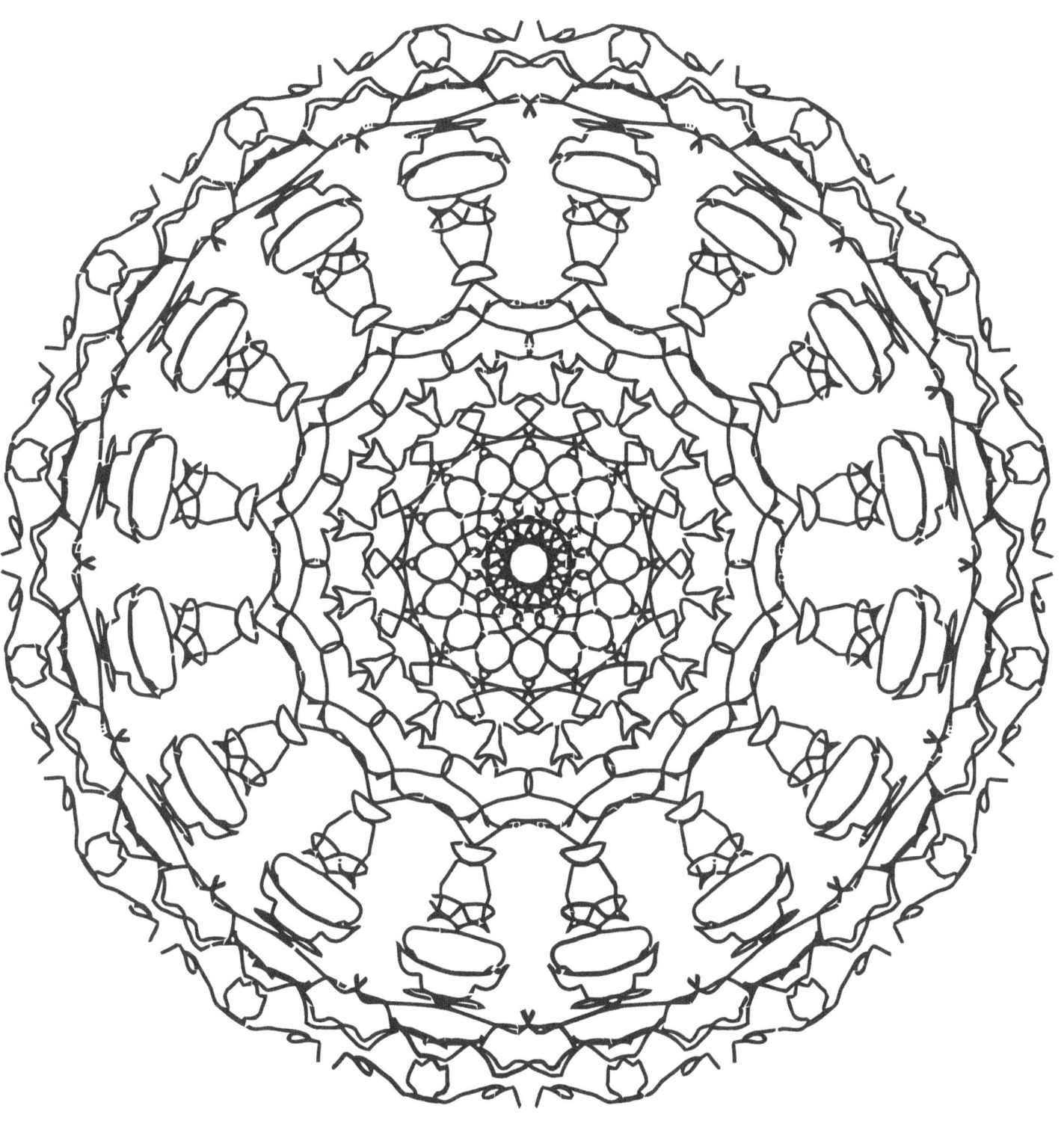

Illustrated by #cherylcolors
www.facebook.com/cherylcolors

Colored by: _____

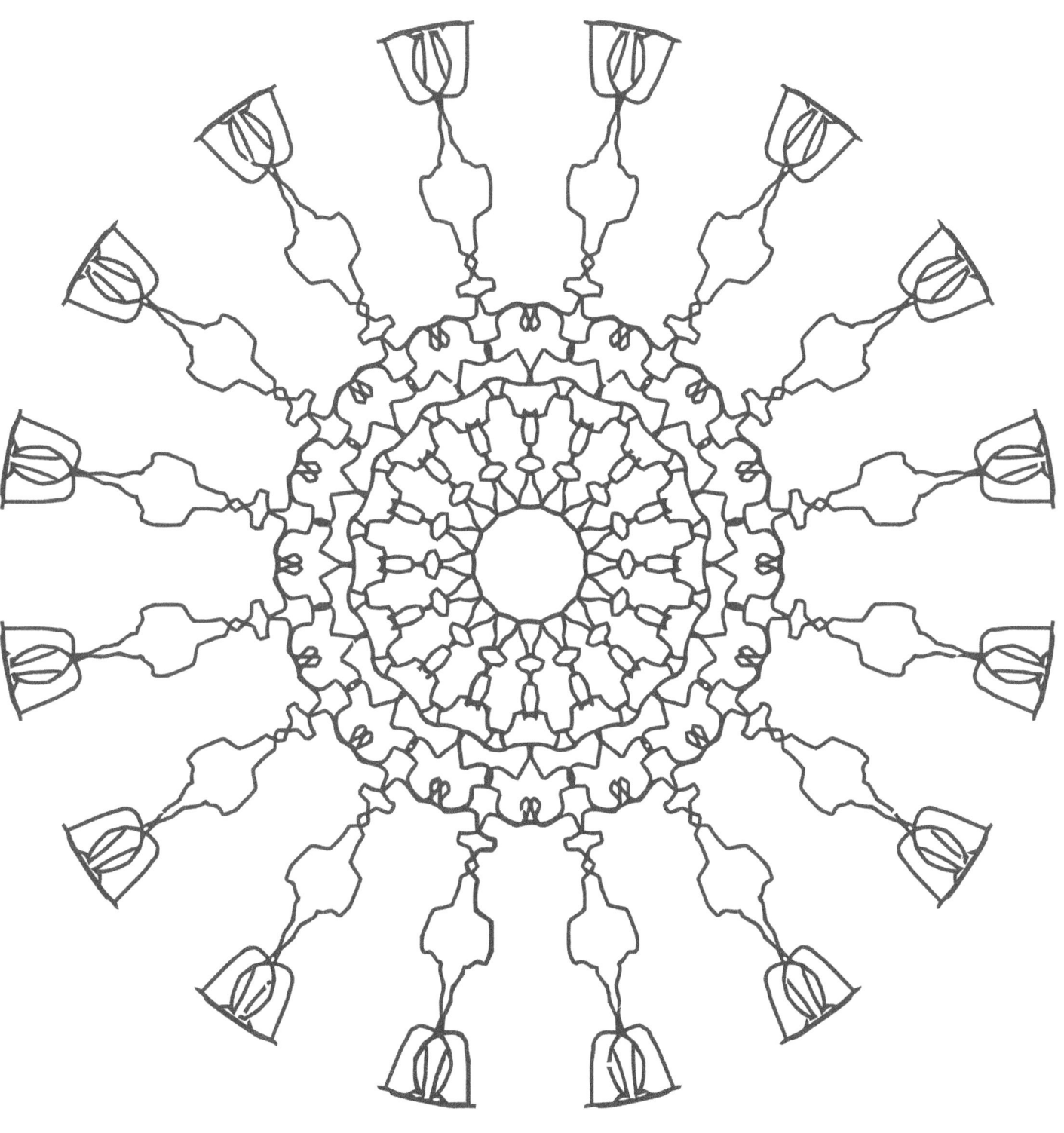

Illustrated by #cherylcolors
www.facebook.com/cherylcolors

Colored by: _____

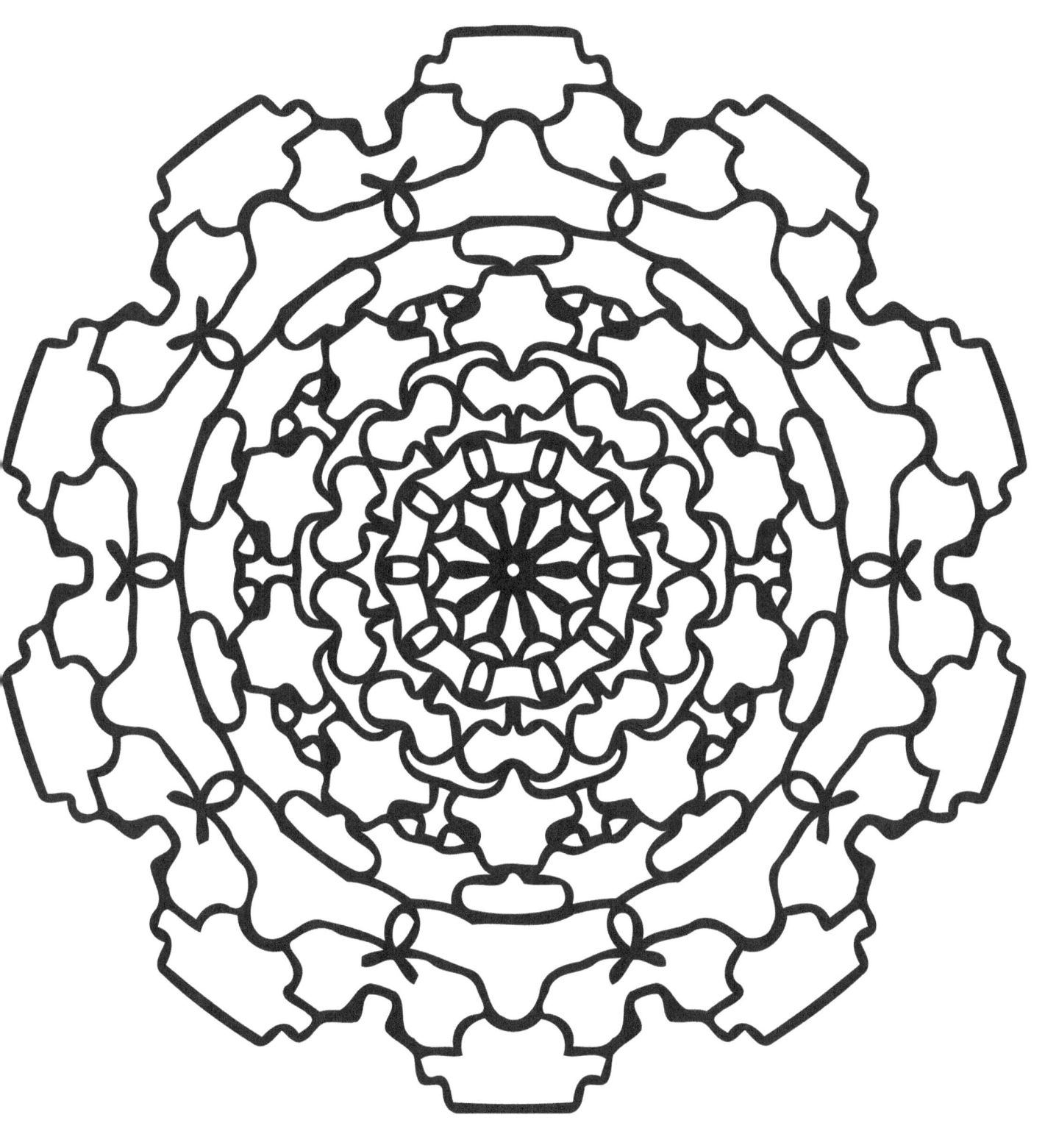

Illustrated by #cherylcolors
www.facebook.com/cherylcolors

Colored by: _____

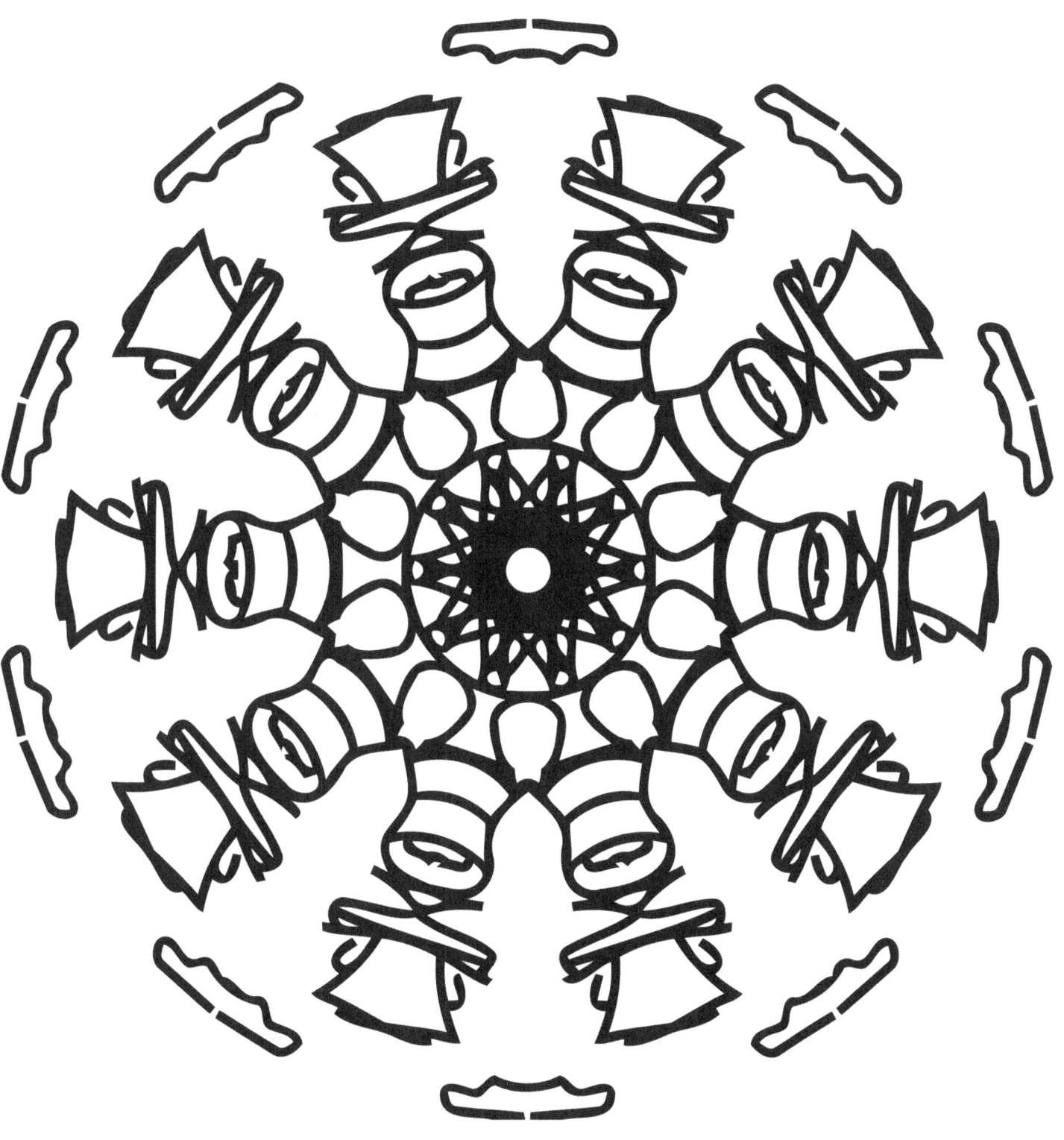

Illustrated by #cherylcolors
www.facebook.com/cherylcolors

Colored by: _____

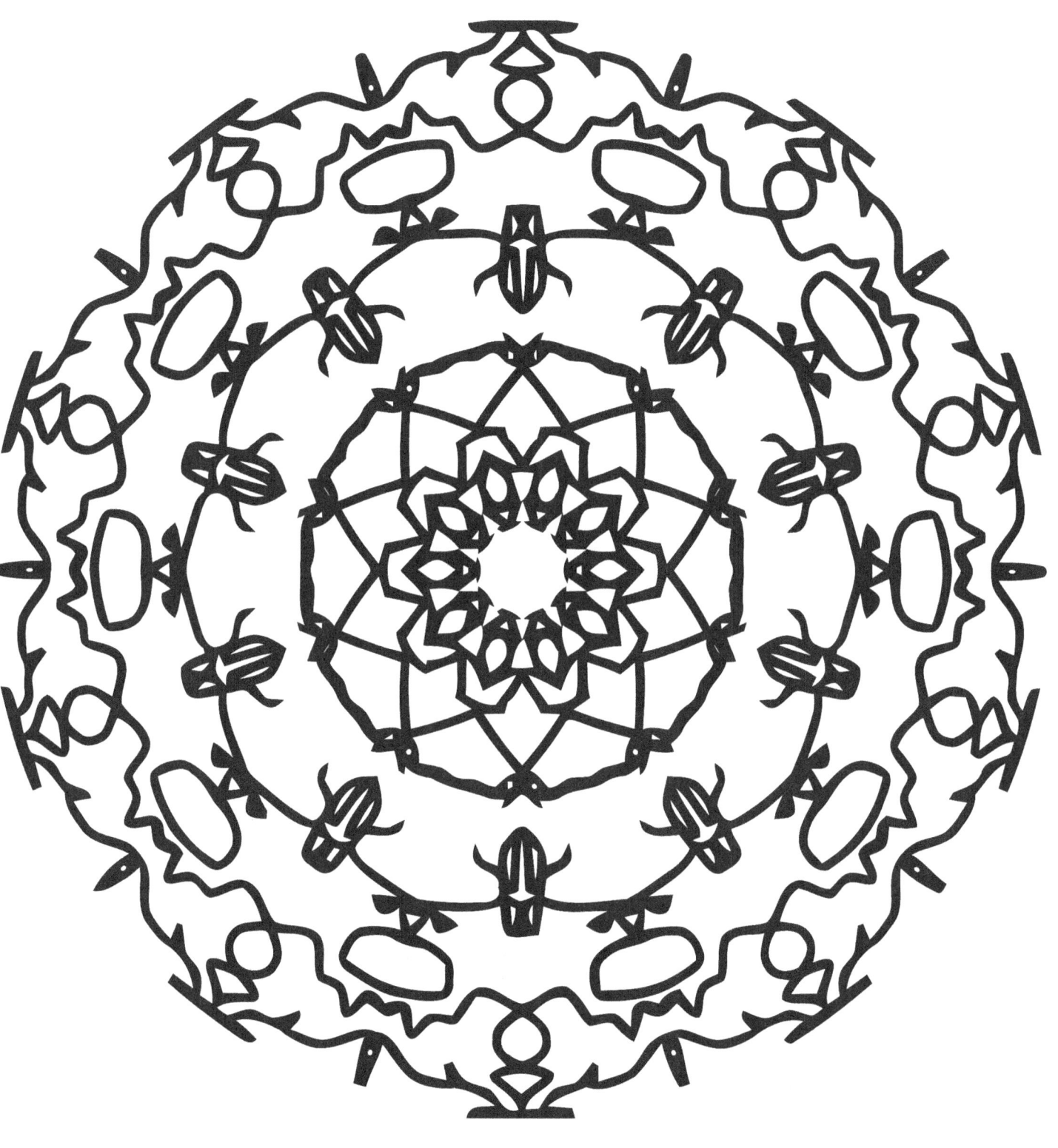

Illustrated by #cherylcolors
www.facebook.com/cherylcolors

Colored by: _____

www.ingramcontent.com/pod-product-compliance
Lightning Source LLC
Chambersburg PA
CBHW082343220526
45470CB00008B/2626